# BATS IN THE BELL TOWER

The following email can be used for any correspondence in regards to this book: batsinthebelltower777@gmail.com.

Book Design & Production:
Columbus Publishing Lab
www.ColumbusPublishingLab.com

Copyright © 2022 by
Kenny Campbell
LCCN: 2022913035

All rights reserved.
This book, or parts thereof, may not be reproduced in any form without permission.

All scripture is quoted from the King James Version Bible unless otherwise noted.

Paperback ISBN: 978-1-63337-642-7
E-Book ISBN: 978-1-63337-647-2

Printed in the United States of America
1 3 5 7 9 10 8 6 4 2

# BATS IN THE BELL TOWER

Unmasking the Doctrines That Have Seduced the Modern-Day Church

Kenny Campbell

This book isn't dedicated to any one person. It is dedicated to a purpose. And that purpose, is God's purpose……….

May it be fulfilled in all who read it.

*Amen.*

*"For this purpose the Son of God was manifested, that He might destroy the works of the devil." 1 John 3:8*

# CONTENTS

Foreword..................................................................1
Introduction............................................................3
Chapter 1: A "God" of Our Own Design................................9
Chapter 2: A Peace Agreement.........................................15
Chapter 3: God, The Great Banker in the Sky.........................25
Chapter 4: Unity at any Cost?........................................37
Chapter 5: A Cold Hard Truth.........................................47
Chapter 6: Position or Possession?..................................59
Chapter 7: A Message to Ministers...................................67
Chapter 8: The Changing of the Guards...............................75
Chapter 9: The Trickle Down Effect..................................83
Chapter 10: Grace: A License?........................................89
Chapter 11: Grace: A Liberation......................................97
Chapter 12: Faith: Fact or Fiction?................................105
Chapter 13: Faith: Evidence or Emptiness?..........................113
Chapter 14: Love: Tolerance or Truth?..............................123
Chapter 15: Psychology: A Brainstorm, or A Brainwash?..............131
Chapter 16: Eternal Security: Favoritism or Farce?.................143
Chapter 17: A Woman of the Night...................................165
Chapter 18: A Matriarch of Municipalities..........................181
Chapter 19: Bats in the Bell Tower.................................193
Chapter 20: A Snuffed Out Candle...................................203
Chapter 21: A Nomad King...........................................211
Chapter 22: The Remnant Rising.....................................223
Epilogue...........................................................235

# FOREWORD

*"Prepare Ye the Way"*

I HEARD THIS PHRASE around 20 years prior to this book coming into existence, and I heard it multiple times. With my thoughts not really being upon God, I would be going about my daily routine as wife and mother, and there it would be again. It was not an audible voice. It came like a call within me, coming from somewhere else, beckoning me. At the time, I didn't fully understand the nature and magnitude of this call, yet, many years later it would be brought back to my memory. This was not just a personal recollection of a verse that I read in the Bible, it was a direct call. John prepared the way of Jesus when He came on the scene in physical form. Now, in these last days, we as believers, are all called upon to prepare the way for the coming of the Lord. The writer of this book is one of those chosen for a specific task much like Jeremiah's "to root out, pull down, and to destroy and to throw down and to build and to plant." This book represents that admonition to the church to get ready by "cleansing itself of all filthiness of the flesh and spirit" in receiving the fullness of Christ. Then shall they, as a result, be the salt of the earth and the lights on many hills.

In His Blessed Service,

Teresa Campbell

Member of the bride of Christ & wife of the author

# INTRODUCTION

*This book was born out of necessity...yet,*
*far from the necessity of a personal need or ambition.*

IT WAS NOT CONCEIVED from the stock of academia nor hatched from the incubator of the learned. The following pages are neither a child of theological exegesis, nor an offspring of seminary semantics. Neither was it formed from a mere dogmatic observation or a personal need to "fix a flat tire," so to speak. No, this is not an attempt to straighten church people out, or an attempt to use a bully pulpit to grind an ax. We are in a much bigger moment than any of these motivations can afford, therefore, it is a moment that calls for much bigger measures. Consequently, this book is a raw, cut to the chase, no bones about it approach to the state of the modern church. My attempt here is to take a bird's eye view of the church's current relevance in the world, whether it be good, or whether it be bad.

Due to the nature and scope of this condition we are about to tackle within these subsequent chapters, you will undoubtedly find this to be one of the most unorthodox books you will ever read. Consequently, if you happen to go beyond this introduction, you may find yourself in a place that you have never been before. Love it or hate it, at some point within these pages, you will discover your need to take a good, hard look in the mirror. This self-examination is far overdue, as the disease of apathy has reached epidemic proportions within the walls of the modern church.

This book is not only designed to challenge your **belief system**, it's also designed to challenge your **belief IN a system.** The intention here is not to squabble over theological janglings. Neither is it an attempt to indict individuals about their lack of proper biblical exegesis. These writings are intended to bypass the head and land squarely upon the heart. Was it not the Lord Himself who stated in Luke 9:44 "Let these sayings *sink* ***down*** into your ears?" Therefore, as you navigate your way through this journey, allow this question to be fostered in your mind: "Do I apply the truth of its pages, or do I disregard it as fanaticism?" That is the only true question you must ask yourself, and consequently, the one question you must come to terms with. So, the only thing that I can ask of the reader is the same thing that the Lord asks of us all, that is, to "Consider your ways" (see Haggai 1:5).

The title of this book came in a moment of great clarity. It came on a particular day when my wife and I were out on a typical trip to the store. As we completed the shopping and loaded back into the vehicle she turned to me and said, "There's something I need to do." I knew she wasn't speaking out of fear, or alarming me of some crisis that she had not yet divulged to me. No, I could tell this was a "surprise" type demeanor she was conveying. I trusted her enough to know that when the Spirit moved her, I was simply going along for the ride. She covertly kept this "something" hidden from me as we drove across town. We then ascended a hill that leads to a local restaurant, one that sits high above our local city. We pulled into the restaurant parking lot and chose a slot next to the long chain link fence that spans the entirety of the property.

# INTRODUCTION

We exited the vehicle and approached the fence whereby we could gaze upon the whole downtown area from a bird's eye perspective.

As we looked out over a city that was oblivious of our very existence and filled with bustling activity, my wife began to pray. As she squeezed my hand tight, she prayed along these lines. "Oh God, you started a work here many years ago and you intend to finish it. Make this place an example of your power to save and deliver from the clutches of hell. We bind those forces over this city that have kept it in chains and loose your great power in the midst of her people, in the mighty name of Jesus."

This prayer came from within. It was not manufactured in the assembly lines of obligatory petition, or prefabricated in her mental faculties. No, this prayer came **FROM** God, and thus went back **UP** to Him! It was indeed a divine thing.

As I gazed out over that city, I saw the many church bell towers extending upwards, almost in an attempt to be the most aesthetically impressive among its peers. I was a bit in awe as to how many of those gothic extensions of religion protruded into the afternoon skyline. The thought then entered my mind, "All these cathedrals, yet still a city given to sin." While standing there, I began noticing the many birds flying about which had made their nests in those pinnacles of piety. That's the very moment when the inspiration came: "Bats in the Bell Tower!"

I had begun this book a couple years prior to this experience. However, I had shelved it in frustration amidst a plethora of other ministerial and occupational commitments. It had yet to receive a title or a definite "theme" at its inception as I had only a couple chapters roughed in. However, this book is far from an afterthought, as it's been over 30 years in the making, germinating in the garden of my soul.

Be assured of this one thing, the Devil hates this book! He hates it simply because it is an exposè of his dark dealings within the modern church. Therefore, it will not be an easy read. You will likely find yourself distracted, badgered, and even quite possibly, attacked in your mind, as you attempt to read it. So, with that said, be prepared at the offset for such diversions to emerge. The kingdom comes with much resistance from hell's gates and only those who press through the crowd can touch God and consequently be touched by Him.

Do not expect this to be a "religiously astute," or, a "politically correct" book. The message contained in these pages will be as far from current religious dogma and ecumenical thinking as night is from day. When I speak of "*religion*" within these pages, I will generally be referring to the word in the sense of mankind's **own efforts** to reach God, and to **please Him** within their **own** perceivings of His requirements. Although the phrase, "Christianity is not a religion, it's a relationship" is heard often in Christiandome, it is actually somewhat misleading to those we are speaking with. By definition of the word *religion* (The service and worship of God or the supernatural), Christianity is most definitely a religion. However, it is the religion of the **heart**, and not of the **head**. This is the ultimate distinction that this book will attempt to draw out into the light.

I have also refrained from mentioning religious figures of the day, and those of yesteryear, except for maybe a thought or two from some that I consider to be godly men. I will also withhold from the use of denominational names, except when necessary for emphasis. However, it will be clear enough in the context as to whether a thought applies to those organizations or not. This book is not written to receive any literary awards, but to rightly divide the fallacy from the truth.

Another anomaly that you will find quite unusual is the position from which I am writing this book. I know this is the part of the book where I, or someone more important than myself, drones on about me

## INTRODUCTION

and my achievements. However, that would take less than a sentence and would bore even a turtle to death. I have no accolades, no degrees, no endorsements, nor institutional training. Simply put, I have not been **knighted** by any clergical scepter, nor do I have a "manstamp" that qualifies me to move about freely in the religious community. Therefore, I have no fear of offense, for I have nothing to lose but more of myself. The gospel is, by nature, an offensive thing. How can it be otherwise and have an effect at the same time? You will understand this more fully as you digest your way through these pages.

Lastly, although it's not my intention, this book will no doubt make you angry at some point. I fully expect this. You will find that the forces within you as well as the ones without, will never go down without a fight. May you be changed in its reading!

## Chapter 1

# A "GOD" OF OUR OWN DESIGN

*"These things hast thou done, and I kept silence. Thou thoughtest that I was altogether such an one as thyself: but I will reprove thee, and set them in order before thine eyes." Psalm 50:21*

Ask yourself this question…

What do I want from God?

Now, after you have pondered the answer, ask yourself another…

What does God want from me?

Now, if you are truthful with yourself, it's very much possible that you may not have a clear answer to either question. If you do have an answer, it could quite possibly be an incorrect notion that has been developed through years of religious cultivation. Perhaps it's even an idea that was grown in the greenhouse of some religious institution and sold to you as viable, naturally grown, seasonal produce. You may have even picked your flavor of Christian experience from a rolling ***a la carte*** of personal preference from a denominational menu of your choosing. This sort of "form-a-god" thinking is precisely why modern forms of Christianity grow so well in this kind of self-serving sod. The landscape of today's faith-filled farmers markets are ripe with the cultivated crops of carnality.

For the most part, today's Christianity is considered to be relative as to how **IT** fits **YOU**. In these times we live in, the gospel has been propagated to mankind as a tailored suit of sorts, one that has been designed for your personal physique. It lays well on you and its sleeves are appropriate in length. Its trousers have been properly modified to land perfectly on your choice of footwear so as not to appear "frumpy." As a result of these ***alterations***, the attire has been fitly crafted to accommodate ***your*** proportions. You don't have to change a thing about ***yourself***, it only ***appears*** that you have, due to its exacting contours. The outward appearance of neatness conceals the inward disproportionate frame. No matter what lies beneath, as long as it looks good to those around, right? This, in a nutshell, is the likeness of the majority of today's modern Christianity. "Throw a suit on anyone, and it makes them look good!"

Ashamedly, this type of topical treason only produces men and women with "a name that thou livest, yet are dead" (see Revelation 3:1). This is the tragedy of the modern gospel and its ill effects on the human condition…. ***embalming*** humanity with the chemicals of false hope, while they yet stand on their feet.

Let me pause here to say this. When I mention the word Christianity heretofore, please be advised as to precisely what I intend to convey. I am using the term only as it relates to our understanding of religion as we currently know it. I do not wish to imply that the plethora of Christian religions around us, which are named after the name of Jesus, are all true Christianity in any sense. This will be self-evident to you as the book evolves and "true Christianity" will be named as such in order to distinguish it from "modern Christianity." I will also refer much to the "modern church" as it relates to our current spiritual environment, it is a church that has largely morphed with the culture and its trends, thereby earning it this title in this book. It is very important that you see this distinction or this body of work will be in vain to you as a reader.

Please let the reader understand that this indictment does not include the entirety of the church world. There are still small pockets of sincere believers functioning in the light that they have received and walking in it as faithfully as they know how. They only become guilty if they reject ***further light***, that is, once they are exposed to it. This book is not aimed at those individuals, except only to be a guide and a preventive element for any pitfalls that may await them in their endeavors to spiritual fullness. Let it be known that the writer intends **NO** personal attacks on any one individual. Rather, let this simply serve as a general exposé on some of the evils that have crept in unawares into the house of God. It does no one in the church world any good to engage in character assassinations.

In the first few chapters of this book we will attempt to explore some of these things that we may wish to attempt to **extract** from almighty God. We will look at the many ways that an underlying, selfish, and humanistic gospel has insidiously grown its vines over the pulpits of absolute truth. Hopefully, by going down this road, we may take a good hard look at how the modern church has morphed into a customized beast, having a "form of godliness" while remaining mostly powerless.

The writer's only attempt here is to examine those doctrinal elements that have weakened the church and stripped her of her power. These doctrinal leavens have permeated throughout the entirety of the modern church. They have become much like Delilah was to Samson. These devilish doctrineers have swooned the church into cutting its glorious hair and thereby robbing it of its prevailing power with God. Satan has caused the ship of Zion much weariness through a relentless, systematic beating of his waves of compromised messages upon the bows of this great gospel ship. The beating has been so effective that she has questioned her very own chartered course. She is marching to the same tune as in the original garden when man and devil first met. It's that same sweetened song in which the serpent posed at the very dawn of creation when he presented that famous question to Eve, "Did God *really* say?" (see Genesis 3:3).

It has always been Satan's conquest from day one in dealing with man to pervert his view of God. His antics have always been spurned from one of the two extremes of the swinging pendulum. These two perversions will always play out in one way or another to lessen God's holiness and to pervert His mercy.

This perversion of our view of God goes all the way back to the garden. But it plays out most extensively when God was dealing with the collective congregation of Israel in the book of Exodus (see Exodus 16). Oh, how successful was this one called Lucifer in the wilderness with the wayfaring children of Israel! "They have **NOT KNOWN** my ways!" (see Psalm 95:10), lamented the Lord. Satan had robbed them of their perception of a benevolent God and achieved his goal of blinding their eyes to the ways of the Lord, especially in the midst of adversity. Their immediate needs had trumped their long term view. The Devil had deceived them and thus stymied the goal of the Lord to bring them into the better land and into the higher place with Himself. "Focus on your immediate lack of care and your physical poverty!" Satan convincingly declared. Hence, they took the bait and accused God of harshness and apathy toward them. It is the downturned eyes of carnality, looking for the immediate relief of all things uncomfortable, that prevent men from seeing the higher ways of God.

So with all of that established, we must understand that these devilish doctrines have a powerful negative effect on the people of God. Those teachings, which are created and incubated in the boardroom of hell, are designed to subvert the church of Jesus Christ. Satan knew that he could never beat the church with persecution as it only caused it to flourish. The fellowship of Christ's sufferings are just too sweet to the true saint to ever forsake Him over mere physical threats.

When Satan, through Saul of Tarsus (who would later become our beloved apostle Paul), tried to kill the maiden voyage of the young church, it backfired. At the end of Acts chapter 7, Stephen prayed with stones falling upon his head while pleading for the very souls of his killers, Saul being the ringleader. Stephen would pray this prayer as his life faded from this earth, "Lay not this sin to their charge!" (see Acts 7:60). This prayer would ascend into the courts of God, be stored in the incense bowl of heaven, and then be poured out upon Saul's head on the way to Damascus. His immediate conversion was likely the unforeseen result of this final lament of our dear Stephen. As the Holy Spirit pleaded through Stephen for the souls of his very killers, this no doubt allowed Paul to see the otherworldliness of this Christ that would soon **ground him** with a great light.

When Satan saw that it was futile to try and kill the church, he would need to devise another plan. That's when the proverbial "If you can't beat em, join em" weapon was then taken from the desk drawer and used upon the church's vulnerable condition as a young fledgling yet in the nest. The marvelously transformed Paul himself, while grieving over his very own susceptible spiritual children, would later experience this very same sorrow as a now spiritual father. He would cry out the following warning in the book of Acts to the newborn Ephesian church.

> "For I have not shunned to declare unto you all the counsel of God. Take heed therefore unto yourselves, and to all the flock, over which the Holy Ghost hath made you overseers,

to feed the church of God, which He hath purchased with His own blood. For I know this, that after my departing shall grievous wolves enter in among you, not sparing the flock. Also of your own selves shall men arise, speaking perverse things, to draw away disciples after them. Therefore watch, and remember, that by the space of three years I ceased not to warn everyone night and day with tears." (Acts 20: 27-31)

Paul most certainly realized that an ***inside job*** was coming and no doubt the Holy Ghost had pressed this upon him with great emphasis. It is obvious that he saw a time coming when the wolf, fitted with the finest wool, would gain his insidious entry among the faithful.

Just what did Paul see? He most certainly saw the vulnerability of the young flock and the earnestness of the devouring wolves to encroach those fences of truth. If this was his cry 2000 years ago, how much more in these times when doctrinal birds fly at will into the towers of sanctity and make their nests unabated in her bell towers? Paul is gone, Peter is deceased, and the beloved John has passed into glory! Who shall stand guard centuries removed from the freshness of their cherished words of warning?

It is the nature of man that when he gets out of earshot of the cry of caution that he then grows more comfortable. This apathy can intensify even in spite of his vessel moving ever so swiftly towards the mighty waterfalls. May God reawaken true guardians to bring back the truth as the standard, put to flight all doctrinal foul birds, and to drive away the hungry wolves. Let us venture on to see where those breaches appear that have afforded these seductions of sanctity to gain their access.

# Chapter 2

# A PEACE AGREEMENT

*"Peace I leave with you, my peace I give unto you: not as the world giveth, give I unto you. Let not your heart be troubled, neither let it be afraid." John 14:27*

So, LET US BEGIN to answer our first question we had raised in chapter 1.

What do you want from God?

If I were to gather an overall consensus from humanity, it is likely that the number one answer would be: "God, would you please give me peace?" I would venture to say that every soul that is seeking even an idea of God would say this. After all, the world is completely loaded with anything but peace. There is fighting on every side, racial divide, religious turmoil, the "Right" and "Left" battle, nation against nation, kingdom against kingdom, and even team against team. These factional fissures make up the very foundations of modern society and are prevalent throughout its "core value" system. So, in light of the devilish division within the human experience, we can certainly conclude that peace is one of the most coveted and needed dispositions on the planet. Everyone is in want of peace in one form or another.

We must first establish that worldly peace, or as Jesus called it, "Peace as the world giveth," ***does*** exist in one form or another. Is it not evident that false peace is all around us? The worldly system (outside the church) offers peace in many forms.

One only needs to look at the drug epidemic to determine this. This is probably the biggest form of false peace that is offered within the world system. It is the effort of mind altering drugs and alcohol in their attempts to quell the clamoring of our troubled souls that no doubt takes top prize in the false realm of peace. This offer comes from various channels and means. It stems from the rogue street corner, the convenient stores with their stocked coolers, and from much of the medical community in their well staffed offices and waiting rooms.

Although the drug epidemic is largely attributed to our unsecured borders, there are more insidious causations right under our own noses. Unfortunately, even a large portion of the medical community have been beguiled and incentivised by the briefcase-toting salesmen of big pharma. The work has already been done in the mortar and pestle and is assured to **do the trick** for abolishing the inner ills of the human condition through chemical redistribution to the psyche. However, the unfortunate result is a pseudo serenity that has caused a fantastical deception of false euphoria. Not to mention a plethora of side effects that are more alarming than the symptoms they are treating.

Only the gospel of peace can cure the inner turmoil of man. All other means of bringing peace to the human condition is like an attempt to chain a raging pitbull to the doghouse of deception and refrain him from self-destruction and from harming his fellow canines. It's all made of the same formula, it's just that one is wrapped in an **unregulated** tin foil, and one is bottled in **regulated** plastic. When we attempt to alter how a human **thinks** and **feels** with concoctions from the cauldrons of chemical formulations, we are meddling with a realm we have no true rights to enter into. It is *all* embodied in the realm of sorcery known as ***pharmakeía***, which in the Greek means: ***the use of medicine, drugs or spells*** (source: Bible Hub/Strongs #5331). These medicinal alterations of the mind, that only attempt to numb the neurotransmitters, cast an insidious spell upon the hearts of mankind. No matter whether it be clothed in a leather jacket with a skull on the back of it, or, draped in a white coat with a name tag pinned to it, its origin is found in the bewitching of Satan.

Due to our consensual ingestion of these chemicals, we are opening the gates of the demonic realm with them. This is the very reason that nefarious spiritual forces are then employed to lock that soul down in bondage. We then become **hooked** on the **treatment** of our very own narcissism, by adding more narcissism. We give it the nice word of "addiction" so we can **treat** it, but it is none other than bondage. We see daily the toll on humanity that these destructive forces are causing, plunging them into the abyss through their ruthless and lying promises of internal solitude. This law of diminishing return may start with a simple painkiller and exponentially rise from there. Although a "high" can cause one to momentarily escape the harsh reality of the here and now, it will insidiously and incrementally inch one toward the point of no return. This is why the overdose rate exponentially increases by the day. Mankind is in pursuit of a "carrot on the stick" euphoria that he will never obtain. This lust after false peace will continue to plunge humanity into eternal darkness, so long as they insist on pursuing the ultimate temporary high.

Peace is likely the most precious, yet simultaneously, the most rare, personal commodity on the planet. As mankind spins ever so quickly toward his destiny of appearing before a holy God, great lamentation and sadness will mark the day when the sinner finds that all his vain searchings for peace were an exercise in futility. He will one day awaken to the ominous reality that true peace awaited him and was within the grasp of his very own hands. The many times he had heard the bidding of the gospel will be recounted to him as he stands before the judge of all the earth. He will then discover that the Lord had held out His offer of peace to him all the days of his existence, but instead, he burned up his days in pursuit of a pseudo pipe dream. May you not find yourself in such a number dear friend, take the offer while you yet stand on this planet! Pursue the pseudo peace of this life no longer, and embrace the true peace of the gospel message through Jesus Christ.

Now, let's turn to the modern church to explore their answer to such a pressing need for peace. What do **they** hold out for you in exchange for peace? Is it through a church **membership**? Is it an opportunity to be a part of something "bigger than yourself" and just to be a part of a **fellowship**? Is it to feel as though you belong to an **in-crowd** of some kind?

Another appeal that the modern church may extend to you is that you need to "follow your dreams." You must seek God, they claim, so as to find out what dream and purpose that He wants you to pursue. They teach that you should get in line with this dream and that true peace comes when one discovers God's **plan for them** as an individual. This **amendment** to the "Constitution of Christianity" for the "pursuit of happiness" has been a monstrous diversion in the modern church and a pre-occupational carrot on a stick. Have you ever heard this appeal to follow your dreams within the house of God? If you have set foot in a modern house of worship, you have likely heard it in one form or another. There are multifaceted versions of peace offered through the church and I cannot possibly cover them all, but you see the point. What is it that appeals to you? Only you know.

Now, if we may summarize these points, it goes a little something like this (as the majority of the modern church proclaims it): "You need to make peace with our ***group of people*** by joining our ranks." Meaning, accept them and be accepted by them. They may also imply that: "You need to make peace with a certain ***doctrine*** and accept without question what we teach." And finally: "You have to make peace with ***yourself*** and accept the dream that God has placed within *you*."

Now, if I may be candid right here, none of these offers by the modern church are true peace as Jesus intended it, but instead, it is peace "as the world gives" (see John 14:27). These appeals are but to the pride and selfishness of man. They do nothing but exalt ***self-worth*** in an individual and promote an insidious kind of self-importance. Instead of being based on a relationship with God alone, they have blended humanistic philosophy with the divine purpose. The appeal ends up being to the ***soulish*** part of man, and brushes to the side the fact that man's most important aspect of his existence is to glorify his Creator in all things**.** "Whether therefore ye eat, or drink, or whatsoever ye do, do all to the glory of God" (1 Corinthians 10:31).

Let us now attempt to draw a distinction between "the peace as the world gives" and "My peace, I give unto you" (see John 14:27). As we have previously mentioned, the false church system is also full of a plethora of this false peace. If Satan can get you to settle into some comfort zone, short of full repentance and union with God, he has been successful. This is what I call "meeting you in the doorway syndrome." It is here at the entry point into the gospel that the devil's devices are the most cunning. Once he sees that the seeking soul is beginning to press into the kingdom of God, he then amps up his efforts to divert the unsuspecting seeker.

This whole diversionary scheme is devised by Satan in order to settle you down into a false hope, just short of regeneration. This is a hope that is only based in doing something **FOR** God, instead of the true hope that comes when one receives something **FROM** God (i.e. His Spirit). The breadcrumbs of false religion will be strewn across your path in order to set you off course in pursuit of some observance, ordinance, or ritual. Perhaps it's a ***certain way*** you need to be baptized. Maybe it's a certain prayer or pledge you need to utter. It could even be an appeal to observe the old Jewish customs under the "Torah observant" movement, or the "Hebrew roots" movement. These "religious door keepers" are set in place to prevent you from obtaining true gospel hope. They are the agents of Satan who unfortunately, much of the time, wear a suit and tie. This camo of congeniality makes them blend into their surroundings and much harder to spot. And, albeit unknowingly at times, they work for the Devil himself.

The modern church system is one that promises a seat among the faithful, that is, as long as you merely conform to their "good ol' boy club" conditions. I liken it to a ***motorcycle club*** of sorts. It's an "exclusivity complex" that appeals to that need within man to belong to a group of folks with the same interests. There is safety in the numbers and a feeling of comradeship that pulls one into the ranks. Before long, one can find themselves joining up to the ***club***, learning the lingo, the special handshake, and the codes and conducts of the organization. They may even advance to the point of throwing on the club's attire and sporting the "skull and bones" of servitude.

If we go to the word of God we can find these appeals addressed very poignantly and passionately by our dear weeping prophet, Jeremiah. Perhaps this scathing set of verses penned by him in chapter 6 will sum up this dilemma. He addresses with earnestness of the Spirit, Gods abhorrence of a peace offering within a system that merely promotes a ***change of position,*** but not a ***change of heart:***

"For from the least of them even unto the greatest of them every one *is* given to covetousness; and from the prophet even unto the priest every one dealeth falsely. They have healed also the hurt *of the daughter* of my people **SLIGHTLY**, saying, **PEACE, PEACE**; when *there is* **NO PEACE.**" ( Jeremiah 6:13-14)

So, we see that this "healing my people **SLIGHTLY**," has an implication of a false pacifying peace. I think that right here, it is important to call upon the Greek definition to see the importance of what is being implied by the prophet. The word "slightly," as used here, carries an interesting definition. It means, "to be slight, swift or trifling" (source: Bible Hub/Strongs # 7043). The word "trifling" is a standout to me because it implies an unimportant or trivial view of something. So then, if these overseers are "healing the hurt slightly," it would stand to reason that this wound of the soul called *sin*, is not being treated with the right medicinal application. In other words, a **topical** treatment is being applied upon the surface of a far **deeper reaching malady** of the soul.

In Mathews account of the gospel, Jesus makes a paralyzing statement to His disciples. He cuttingly declares: "Do not assume that I have come to bring peace to the earth, but a sword" (see Matthew 10:34). Wow! Imagine His follower's dismay! Here is a group of folks who expect a king of *peace* to come and straighten out a crooked society. They fully expected Him to set things right in a social sense and to place Israel back in charge as the kings of the earth and abolish all opposition to *their* peace. He was after all, the "Prince of peace" (see Isaiah 9:6) as the scriptures foretold, wasn't He?

Let's take a closer look at the statement He made: "Do not assume that I have come to bring peace to the *earth*." Let us observe right here that Jesus never intended to bring peace to the earth as a **whole** (at least not on this first trip). He did not intend to bring peace **to** a particular segment of society. Nor did He attempt to ride into the condition of humanity upon the back of the white stallion of worldly conquest. No, He would enter the city on a lowly donkey and lay down His life in a humiliating relinquishment of His own body. This, He would do, in order to infuse that true peace into the internal temples of mankind. He knew too well that true and lasting peace could never come to this cold, dead planet in which Satan, "The god of this world, hath blinded, lest the light…..should shine unto them." (see 2 Corinthians 4:4). Jesus operated under no such delusion as He knew this world remains under the curse of disobedience until the determined future. Then, and only then, shall He come upon that white horse to set all things righteous! (see Revelation 19:11).

In His passage in Matthew, the Lord gives a prophetic hint into the dividing essence of the gospel message. This message of "division by default" would even penetrate into the common household. Jesus would forewarn His disciples that the gospel, when wholly embraced, would separate out the basic passions of humanity. This dividing sword of truth would be drawn and cut to the quick of our soul in order to draw the distinctive line between the kingdom of this world, and the kingdom of God. Insomuch that even those who were once our dear comrades and endearing familial attachments, would find our new found passion for all things righteous to be repulsive to them.

As we clearly see by these conclusions, that the form of peace that Jesus spoke of here could not have been just *relative* to our environment. Neither could He have been trying to teach us to simply "get along in the world." No, this is a different kind of peace that Jesus spoke of. This peace can be no less than the peace of reconciliation *to* God!!!

# A PEACE AGREEMENT

In John 14:27, Jesus would say it like this, "My peace I leave with you, my peace I give to you. I do not give to you as the world gives."

Here we see that the difference is an actual ***transaction*** of sorts, a passing from one to another and something given ***by God to man***. He can only be referencing His very own Spirit. We recall how He "breathed" on them His Spirit right after His resurrection (see John 20:22). This was, no doubt, an earnest ***down payment***, until He could ascend to the throne and send forth His Spirit at Pentecost. He knew if a deposit were not left, they would never hold out until then. So wise is this God!

We should also consider another truth concerning the subject of peace. What is its origin and purpose for its existence in our soul? Paul, in his epistle to the Philippians, addressed it this way:

> "Be careful for nothing; but in every thing by prayer and supplication with thanksgiving let your requests be made known unto God. And the peace of God, which **PASSETH ALL UNDERSTANDING**, shall keep your hearts and minds through Christ Jesus." (Philippians 4:6-7)

Allow us to take note that this is a peace that does not find its lodging in the intellect, nor is it a ***resolution*** of the mental faculties. Neither can it be self-induced, or pushed upon you by convincing clergy and motivational speakers who talk you into a better sense of it. No, it will not come this way at all. Never! This peace comes to the **HEART**! It is exclusively the result of a true union of God and man through the reconciliatory blood of Jesus, and His atoning work on the tree. You simply cannot experience this genuine peace until an actual repentance from sin, and a ***RECEIVING*** of Christ into the heart has occurred. I dearly love these verses in Colossians chapter 1, they certainly tell the story:

> "For it pleased *the Father* that in Him should all fullness dwell; And, having made **PEACE** through the blood of His cross, by Him to **RECONCILE** all things unto Himself; by Him, *I say*, whether *they be* things in earth, or things in heaven. (Colossians 1:19-20)

The conclusion of this matter is simple. It is the fact that nothing short of reconciliation with God can bring true peace and that all else is man-made attempts at personal serenity. Also, take note that the nature of the reconciliation is **unto Himself**, implying a complete union of our spirit with His Spirit. So in other words, it is a cohabitation of the **Peacemaker** with His lost, tempestuous creatures. I write the following statement with great conviction. There is no peace outside of reconciliation, and there is no reconciliation without a full and complete giving up of ourselves to Him.

Clearly, we see that peace comes through surrender of our hostile will up to God's will, and not God simply arbitrarily bestowing it upon the half-hearted appeal of our hearts. The gospel was never good news because it makes us *feel better*, but it is good news because it lets us back in behind the veil of the most holy place to sup with Jesus Himself. The peace of God, is union with God, and anything short of this will be a peace that should be considered an **imposter.**

I will simply end this chapter with Paul's words:

> "Therefore we are ambassadors for Christ as though God did beseech you by us, we pray for you on behalf of Christ, be ye reconciled to God!" (2 Corinthians 5:20)

Chapter 3

# GOD, THE GREAT BANKER IN THE SKY

*"A little that a righteous man hath is better than
the riches of many wicked." Psalm 37:16*

IN THIS AGE OF GREAT ABUNDANCE, we must not fail to mention something else that one might desire of God…….

Prosperity.

At no other time in history have we seen such passion for "stuff." The surmounting debt of the nation, of individuals, and of the common household, can attest to nothing otherwise. Due to our unbridled passion "to have and to hold" all things that our heart desires, we are no doubt running down the slick rails of utter bankruptcy. Our train to financial destruction has no brakes except for an inevitable wall of fiscal failure. We have erected this plastic castle out of fiat fakery and it will soon topple, while humanity will be left to pick up the pieces the best that they can. They will then be forced to try and glue them back together in order to just get by. It will be then, and only then, that they will fully know that it has all been a sham. The time bandit of their souls, Satan, had preoccupied them in order to keep them away from the true spiritual riches in Christ Jesus.

Allow me right here to make an important point. This lust for things does not necessarily have to do with just the actual **possession** of anything. Covetousness has within its definition the lusting **after** something. It does not necessarily imply the ownership of all things worldly, but also a **passion to obtain** such things. Greed, however, would imply the ownership of the property and the withholding of it to all others who may be in more need of it. So we see here that we are dealing with two different passions that are cut out of the same mold. I know people who are of both camps and therefore possess both vices. But I also know some who don't have the **means** to obtain that which they lust for, yet their longing for it consumes them. Both sins stem from "The lust of the flesh, the lust of the eyes, and the pride of life" (see 1 John 2:16). The first being the lust to **experience** it, the second being the lust to **obtain** it, and the third being the **hoarding** of it after taking possession. I think the apostle James said it well in the fourth chapter of his short yet poignant letter, concerning those **WITHIN THE CHURCH** who returned to such carnality. This desire for prosperity and position would even permeate through their very own prayers!

> "From whence **come** wars and fightings among you? **Come they** not hence, **even of your lusts** that war in your members? Ye lust, and have not: ye kill, and desire to have, and cannot obtain: ye fight and war, yet ye have not, because ye ask not. Ye ask, and receive not, because ye ask amiss, that ye may consume *it* upon your lusts. Ye adulterers and adulteresses, know ye not that the friendship of the world is enmity with God? Whosoever therefore will be a friend of the world is the enemy of God." (James 4:1-4)

If you were to turn on religious broadcasting right now, you would likely see that it's awash with flagrant displays of ministerial merchandise. These are Pentecostal pushers who are selling religious relics and bombarding us with books and peddling nearly every trinket and charm that you can glue a cross to. These "pulpiteers" cast their lures into the sea of souls in order to reel in their funds from the unsuspecting fish. Yet, far worse than the lure, is what they offer in return for those funds! It is an opportunity to be a part of the system of "God's best," where continual prosperity flows down the mountain like honey, into your awaiting trenches of expectancy.

For the sake of time and space, I need not go into an explanation of the depths of the so-called "Prosperity Movement." Nor do we need to delve into its origin, its evolution to its current status, or its eventual and certain death. This doctrine has done much harm and has sidetracked multitudes of young believers from the true pursuit of God. It is a sad fact that many newborn believers have fallen prey to this doctrine soon after their conversion. I personally believe it to be one of the most effective diversionary doctrines in history.

Satan's number one goal is to derail the newborn Christian by one means or another. His first attempt is to pull the newborn believer back into the world with some of the more recent temptations that are relative to their old sins. The young believer is most vulnerable to those things they have just freshly departed from, due their proximity and availability for the devil's use against them (i.e. drink, drugs, sexual sins, anger, greed). If Satan sees that this enticement is futile, and that the newborn soul is going to stick with their new-found freedom, he then begins to try to turn the soul inward through a systematic relentless appeal of a subtle selfishness.

Allow me to explain. When a soul is let out entirely to God, washed by the blood of Jesus and cleansed from their past, only then can they see clearly. They then realize that it's all about God's glory **within them** and the soul gushes forth outwardly to God and His mercy. The inward eyesight, with scales now removed, looks steadfastly on the vast display of love and forgiveness in the cross. In the shock and awe of this new found reality, the soul asks: "How could He, why would He, how did He endure all this suffering for me?" These newly discovered sensibilities rush as torrents from within us as an elated expression of thanksgiving. The overwhelming reality now takes possession of the soul and it is all outward to God. One's affection then becomes entirely upwards toward the Lord Himself, catapulting them into a selfless state of mind.

But then he comes, that great serpent called the Devil, deceiving as he comes. And, unfortunately he is wearing a suit and tie, and carrying a Bible. This certainly makes him hard to spot, doesn't it? But his message always has the same intent even though his tactics may differ at times. It is his goal to turn the soul back *inward* and back to the focus of *self* once again. If he succeeds, he will bring one to a place where they will say something like this: "God is all about making me happy and satisfied, and He reigns in heaven for the betterment of mankind." Satan will throw all the "prosperity" Bible verses at that soul to validate this claim and to try and turn them back to a self-serving state. He will quote such verses as "I wish above all things that you would *prosper* and that you would be in health" (see 3 John 1:2), along with other verses that pertain to "blessings." These are in fact legitimate verses, but it is their *misuse* that poses the danger and not the verses themselves. Through these types of verses, coupled with the "ministers of merchandise," he will continually bombard their souls until their thoughts are turned like a great ship, back to the shores of selfishness.

This persuasion could take some time, but the lion is patient and will wait out the moment. Before one realizes it, they will find themselves falling in line with all the other self-serving followers of this doctrine of devils. Consequently, they will miss out on the fullness of Christ by pursuing one's own self-interest with a perceived stamp of God's approval on it. Their seeking of God has now become "earthly, sensual, and devilish" (see James 3:15). Once they believe this ideology, God has then become their divine "banker." He is then visited only in the time of need for a withdrawal from His great bank in the sky. Slowly, He becomes much like their earthly financier in which they may happen to pass by at the mall or bump into at a restaurant.

Much like that banker, God then becomes a casual acquaintance and that individual loses that intimate desire of getting to know Him ***personally***. Over time, they find themselves approaching God less and less for the reason of getting to ***know*** him, and more about what they can ***withdraw*** from Him. Their prayers then become petitions of prosperity instead of groanings of gratitude. Alas, Satan has achieved his goal and has turned the gospel into something that serves only ***themselves*** in their self-induced pilgrimage through this life. This alternative view of the Lord becomes their focus, diverting their heart and life from being laid down as a living sacrifice for the Lord Jesus, to a self-absorbed abuser of God's grace.

I spoke earlier of the misuse of certain scriptures, namely the ones that Satan uses to promote a selfish gospel in their ear. Conversely, allow me now to mention a set of verses that can hardly be twisted, due to their straightforward message. Paul, in the first book of Timothy, lays this subject of wealth out quite clearly:

> "Perverse disputings of men of corrupt minds, and destitute of the truth, supposing that ***gain*** is ***godliness***: from such withdraw thyself. But godliness with ***contentment*** is great gain. For we brought nothing into *this* world, *and it is* certain we can carry nothing out. And having food and raiment let us be

therewith **content**. But they, that will be rich, fall into temptation and a snare, and *into* many foolish and hurtful lusts, which drown men in destruction and perdition. For the love of money is the root of all evil: which while some coveted after, they have erred from the faith, and pierced themselves through with many sorrows. But thou, O man of God, flee these things; and follow after righteousness, godliness, faith, love, patience, meekness." (1 Timothy 6:5-11)

So then, we must ask ourselves, what is "godliness with contentment?" Here, I must again indulge in a bit of the Greek. I think this definition of **contentment** is a wonderful expression as to the intended thought of the apostle in this passage.

> Contentment = properly, self-sufficient; used of the Spirit-filled Christian – having all they need within, through the indwelling Christ. (source: Bible Hub/Strongs# 841)

Plainly, we can see that what is being expressed here by the word contentment is the absolute satisfaction of the soul due to the cohabitation of the Spirit of Christ with our spirit. This alone is sufficient to render unnecessary, all other lovers within our human spirit. It literally drives a javelin through the heart of the materialistic lusts that have so often been elevated in the modern church as part of the gospel "blessings." This insidious association of material items, being thus equated to the blessings of God, has done much damage to the modern Church.

Now, before you close this book and walk away peeved over what you have just read, allow me to be clear. Is it a ***blessing*** to have a new pair of shoes when your toes are falling out of your other ones? Is it a ***blessing*** to receive a hot meal when you are in great hunger? Is it a ***blessing*** to be able to pay a bill that you otherwise would not have been able to, had someone not been led by God to put a fistful of cash in your hand? Certainly these are ***good things*** and they do afford small popcorn moments of elation, but, therein lies the problem within this modern doctrine.

In the modern church, we have erroneously made the unfortunate association of these types of "blessings" as the verification of our favor with God. In other words, if you are impoverished, can't pay a bill, or you suffer some type of malady, it is almost always assumed that you are out of the favor of God. But, as the apostle was trying to bring across so very clearly in the passage, it is the inner contentment that sustains one in all conditions, whether poverty or plenty. In fact, it was Jesus Himself who would bring to attention the universal blessings upon all of humanity, based on nothing of merit, but simply that God is intrinsically good.

> "That ye may be the children of your Father which is in heaven: for He maketh His sun to rise on the evil and on the good, and sendeth rain on the just and on the unjust." (Matthew 5:45)

The Christian should be so endued with the Spirit of God, that in any circumstance, they are able to maintain the same level of satisfaction in the soul. Riches cannot touch it, neither can they persuade it, nor can they be moved from their solid place of love for God. Conversely, poverty can by no means sway the soul from the determination that God is good in all things, and that His love is consistent based on nothing that affects this earthly body, good or bad. His nature always remains just and His providence smothered in divine wisdom.

As we noted by those passages in Timothy, Paul emphasizes the distinction between the temporary and the eternal. He points out the fact that contentment in our walk with God is from a pure, unadulterated relationship which is priceless and has no material connection to it. It's beyond clear in these passages that Paul is highly discouraging the pursuit of all things worldly. He is in fact proclaiming that mere bare necessities are enough for the spiritually contented soul (i.e. food and raiment).

Now, before folks walk out on this book and assume that the writer is suggesting that all should walk around as nomads, scrounging in dumpsters and wearing rags, allow us to clarify. I do not believe that Paul was here suggesting this notion of abject poverty being acquainted with holiness, as we will see later in another passage. I do believe, however, that he was promoting a lifestyle of simplicity. He was clearly touching on the dangers of **PURSUING** materialism as a means of **SATISFACTION**. Material blessings may undoubtedly come into the saint's life, but they should never be able to touch the nerves of his soul. Many times they are bestowed on us in order to simply pass them into the hands of a more needful brother or sister. We can see it clearly in this passage in the second chapter of the book of Acts:

> "And all that believed were together, and had all ***things common***; And sold their possessions and goods, and parted them to ***all men***, as every man ***had need***." (Acts 2:44-45)

This social solidarity was the result of the Holy Ghost subduing the hearts of believers and filling them with the selfless love of God. When the love of God flows forth into the heart, material connections simply melt into oblivion. It's then that one willingly unhands anything that would deprive his less fortunate brethren of a need, while he himself holds excess in his possession. They will even go to the point of selling their unnecessary possessions to make up for the lack in their brothers and sisters. The apostle John reiterates this thought in his small, yet powerful epistle.

> "But whoso hath this world's good, and seeth his brother have need, and shutteth up his bowels of compassion from him, how dwelleth the love of God in him?" (1 John 3:17)

Here, John makes a cutting statement, and I paraphrase: "How is it that you possess excess, and your brother goes without? This simply cannot be." It becomes evident by this verse that the love of God cannot possibly abide in one's bosom, if that person with insolence, can turn away a need. To withhold from a brother in need is to insult the very foundational principles of Christianity. As a true believer, it's simply not possible to saunter past a necessity within the body of Christ and pay it no regard. This lack of action without, testifies to the void within.

It is a most glorious day when the Christian can see that their walk with God is uncircumstantial and that it's in no way connected to temporal benefits. Conversely, it is also a victorious thought to realize that material scarcity cannot discompose the true believer as long as they cling tightly to their divine provider. The Christian that is full of God will find their walk to be the same even keel in all conditions. Being dead to prosperity and equally dead to poverty, is a marvelous, steadfast position with God. This is the thought that our dear apostle Paul brings to life in his letter to the Phillipians:

> "Not that I speak in respect of **want**: for I have learned, in whatsoever state I am, **therewith** to be content. I know **both** how to be **abased** (humbled), and I know how to **abound**: everywhere and in all things I am instructed both to be full and to be hungry, both to abound and to suffer need. I can do all things through Christ which strengtheneth me." (Philippians 4:11-13)

Here, the apostle established the precedent, "Whether feast or famine, I am not moved! My walk with Christ is one of inner sustenance! I am eating of the manna of the Spirit and I am drinking from the Rock that follows me! I am not in want, though my outward man perishes. I have been supplied by the supply of the Spirit within."

Even our Lord Himself spoke on this wise when His disciples took notice of the scarcity of food that He partook of. So much was their concern for His health that in the 4th chapter of John they attempted to urge Him to eat. His answer fell upon carnal ears, though He gave it nonetheless.

> "In the meanwhile, His disciples prayed Him, saying, 'Master, eat.' But He said unto them, 'I have meat to eat that ye know not of.'" (John 4:31-32)

He then proceeds in His attempt to show them that His true sustenance was the will of the Father, and not natural food. Basically His answer went something like this, if I may paraphrase here: "I do not have much use for the basics of carnality for I am so impassioned with my mission that I can but very little look to my own earthly needs. I cannot focus on the temporal needs of this life, saving only to the point that it is necessary to survive."

Our wonderful Lord and Savior lived just such a life of contentment. He lived on such meager means, even to the point of getting His tax money out of the fish's mouth! (see Matthew 17:27) Oh, what a dependency on His father! Their very food came from the exact placement of a fisher's net that was led by the Spirit of God as to where it should land on the surface of the water! (see John 21:6).

Jesus was here on a mission. That mission was the redemption of mankind. He would spend no time outside of that which was necessary in such trivialities of the flesh. He knew that His body was expendable and that it was going to be placed upon a tree and mangled beyond comprehension. He understood it as a vehicle, nothing more, nothing less. It would be the means by which God would reconcile the world. He would then be able to come back as an eternal Spirit and dwell in countless tabernacles, even our very bodies! Therefore, He never coddled it, He never pampered it, and He never viewed it as a permanent tabernacle.

The Lord never tried to amass any form of wealth regarding that tabernacle and He barely even ate at times. He was drawing from the nutrients of the kingdom! His Father was supplying Him with the graces of the inner sustenance. Oh what devotion, oh what tenacity, oh what drive! Pushing away the plate of the world in order to go and die the death for all! No greater love is there than this!

When the believer discovers this sustaining flow and walks therein, how marvelous the satisfaction! How fulfilling to be consumed by God! How glorious to be enamored with His virtue. May we see it, may we want it, may we have it! May we live there always. That old hymn of Helen Howarth Lemmel says it well!

> Turn yours eyes upon Jesus
> Look full in His wonderful face
> And the things of earth
> Will grow strangely dim
> In the light of His glory and grace.

May we learn contentment in this pilgrimage, and loosen our grip on this life, for "The fashion of this world passeth away" (see 1 Corinthians 7:31). I will simply allow the apostle Paul and the prophet Habbakuk to take us out of this chapter:

"If ye then be risen with Christ, seek those things which are above, where Christ sitteth on the right hand of God. Set your affection on things above, not on things on the earth. For ye are dead, and your life is hid with Christ in God. When Christ, *who is* our life, shall appear, then shall ye also appear with Him in glory." (Colossians 3:1-3)

"Although the fig tree shall not blossom, neither *shall* fruit *be* in the vines; the labor of the olive shall fail, and the fields shall yield no meat; the flock shall be cut off from the fold, and *there shall be* no herd in the stalls: Yet I will rejoice in the LORD, I will joy in the God of my salvation." (Habakkuk 3:17-18)

Chapter 4

# UNITY AT ANY COST?

*"Endeavoring to keep the unity
of the Spirit in the bond of peace." Ephesians 4:3*

If we are to continue down our list of things desired from God, then we must certainly include **unity** in the running. Is it not the anthem of the masses? Do we not continually hear the cry within, as well as without the religious establishment? If you were to hang around religious circles long enough, you would hear these subtle cries emitting from within her core: "Can't we all just get along? Can't we just agree to disagree? Don't all roads lead to one? Do not all rainbows end in the same pot of gold? Aren't we all just one great big body anyhow? As long as we all believe in Jesus, we're good, right?" This is the cry that ascends from the mouth of the **ecumenical monster** that is hiding under the pews of the modern church.

In light of the aforementioned dilemma, there exists a strange dichotomy that I must mention right here. While Satan tries to bring together his many doctrinal entanglements into one blender, he simultaneously attempts to divide and isolate the true remnant of Christ from one another.

Depending on which definition that one refers to, this word

*ecumenism* can take on a couple of different meanings. For the sake of this chapter I will simply use the following explanation:

> Ecumenism: the principle or aim of promoting **unity** among the world's Christian churches. (source: Lexico/ UK Dictionary)

We see an ideology here in this definition, whether practical or hypothetical, that somehow unity can be achieved through blending together the many doctrinal divisions that flourish in modern Christianity. It plays out in conferences, it manifests on a host of religious internet sites, and even prevails among many local assemblies. Satan relishes the thought of unity so long as his doctrinal foul birds can still fly among the crowds, defiling their unsuspecting victims with their insidious doctrines.

Some may say that **DIVISION** has been the deepest wound of the modern church. However, I would argue that **UNITY** has been its most damaging blow. Yet, both conditions can be equally fatal, or equally beneficial, depending on the *spirit* and *motivation* of the attempt. The unity in which we see in Ephesians 4 (the passage we alluded to at the offset), must be wrought by the **Spirit of God** or it cannot be authentic unity. If it is not that *divine kind* of unity, it will no doubt drip with the nectar of man-made ideologies and false peace. We the church cannot unify falsities to promote truth. This is a fatalistic idea, and has no doubt driven a spear through the heart of the church. Since the body of Jesus Christ has absolute truth at its core, it cannot deviate from that truth, as it would destabilize its very foundation.

In 325 A.D., an emperor of Rome known as Constantine would make this futile attempt of unity at what is known as the **Council of Nicea**. Through doctrinal decree and legislative powers he sought to encapsulate all of Christiandome within one manageable form. We cannot be sure if this motivation stemmed from a political objective, or from his own

Christian interests, God only knows what the true answer to that question is.

Regardless of the motive, the outcome would be a blueprint for unity sought through human endeavors and would haunt the church until this very day. The emperor would take it upon **himself,** along with the help of the religious dignitaries of the day, to bring about a prescribed oneness under the banner of government. This attempt to draw the faith in tight under the umbrella of ecumenical easement, was as unsuccessful as trying to chain up lighting with a nylon cord. The results, although likely unbeknownst to the perpetrators, were catastrophic to the faith. This spiritual orgy of carnal canonizing created a vacuum of spiritual whoredom which would permeate down through the church age as a leaven.

Many today, as well as throughout the preceding centuries, would herald this effort as noble and view it as a valid attempt to bring spiritual peace to the masses. However, this endeavor backfired and inevitably created a vacuum of division and an *aloof* mentality among the most "pious." An unforeseen precedent would proceed out of this attempt to unionize human reasoning with the wonderment of the inner revelation of Jesus Christ. It would inevitably create an artificial gap between pulpit and pew, and elevate the clergy to undue exaltations in the mind of the common laity.

It would become the catalyst for the heady and high minded models of interpretation, and hierarchical disconnect, that we still employ to this day.

Countless hours were spent by these men, hashing out the doctrine of the Trinity, the advent of Easter, and other doctrinal disputes. As these men employed *reasoning* over *revelation*, an abyss was opened from beneath, and the second heavens fell in our midst with all its afforded doctrinal devils.

Division, although frowned upon by most, can be a very advantageous thing. God is always separating out a **remnant**. He is ever dividing it from the flock of "easy believism" in order to take it further up the mountain in the revelation of Himself. Here, those hungry sheep can graze on peaceful plateaus where wolves struggle due to their lack of ability to contend with the more sure footing afforded to the flocks. Separation and division are good, if its purpose is to isolate the more ardent pursuers of God from the more content grazers. Their submission to God's full plan and purpose equip these particular sheep with an authority that the common **church member** does not enter into. "**Submit** yourselves therefore to God. **Resist** the devil, and he will *flee* from you." (James 4:7)

Unity, as the modern church perceives it, will never be achieved by merely pulling up a chair next to the lukewarm and religiously content while hoping for the temperature of our passion to automatically go up. We must lead one another further up to the heights of God, while being always in pursuit of a fuller view of the Lord. This, we must continually do in order for Christ to have the preeminence in all things. "Exhort one another daily, as long as it is called today" (see Hebrews 3:13).

Let us walk away from the common denominator of fruitlessness and press further into the vineyard of God. May we press past the plateaus of pretense and push upward to the peaks of perfection in Christ. Ecumenism is the broken leg of the ascending sheep, only impairing and impeding their drive to go higher up the mount of God. Let us make our anthem, "Sir, we would see Jesus!" (see John 12:21). May we not rest until all that God can afford to give us of His spiritual riches in Christ Jesus, has been obtained. Let us not be pampered with the pleas of easy believism, nor allow ourselves to be cushioned on the couch of compromise! We cannot hope to cling to the frayed rope of false unity! Rather, let us be twisted together by the binding threads of truth! Paul's statement in 1st Corinthians gives us the blueprint in establishing true unity:

> "I appeal to you, brothers and sisters, in the name of our Lord Jesus Christ, that you all speak the **same thing**, and there be **no divisions** among you, but that you are perfectly joined together in the **same mind**, and the **same judgment**."
> (1 Corinthians 1:10)

Truly, we should consider a few questions in light of this verse. Is Paul here proclaiming a pipe dream? Is he holding out a carrot on a stick? Is it just some fantastical assumption that true unity is possible? Or, is it more feasible to assume that true unity, that is free of compromise, is possible? I think the latter must apply here, seeing that Paul never set forth such false notions. So, if true unity is the end, then what must be the means?

The powers of hell are well aware of the dangers of true unity. Their kingdom is still shaking after the Pentecostal plundering they took at the outpouring of the Holy Ghost at the very founding of the New Testament church. The forces of darkness have already witnessed and experienced the results of an, "All in one accord in one place" scenario in Acts 2:1. From that day, until now, those powers have sought to prevent themselves from ever taking such a beating again.

Due to its rare appearance, unity in the Spirit is very hard for the modern church to recognize. It is unfortunately a fleeting thought and a road largely untraveled by its misled masses. Much to the delight of Satan, the heralders of a hollow harmony are trying to find a way to bridge the divide through fleshly means. Meanwhile, the Spirit of God works tirelessly to bring about that true unity through the binding cords of truth.

Spiritual unity is indeed possible, but it cannot come through the channels of compromise. There can be but one criteria, and that is the love of God manifested in the Spirit of truth. This alone can be the tie that binds His beloved children together. When the cries of the children of God ascend with one unified tune, it is only then that these notes enter into the holy place and consequently into the ears of God. That cry must be filtered down to a unique singleness. This fragrance of frailty must break forth from the children of God and must translate to an, "Avenge us of our adversary" lamentation. This is the same earnest plea that came from the persistent widow in the parable that Jesus lays out for us in the Gospel of Luke:

> "And he spake a parable unto them *to this end*, that men ought always to pray, and not to faint; Saying, There was in a city a judge, which feared not God, neither regarded man: And there was a widow in that city; and she came unto him, saying, Avenge me of mine adversary. And he would not for a while: but afterward he said within himself, Though I fear not God, nor regard man; Yet because this widow troubleth me, I will avenge her, lest by her continual coming she weary me. And the Lord said, Hear what the unjust judge saith. And shall not God avenge His own elect, which cry day and night unto Him, though He bear long with them? I tell you that He will avenge them speedily. Nevertheless when the Son of man cometh, shall He find faith on the earth?" (Luke chapter 18:1-8).

Many may see this adversary in verse three as being a type of the Devil himself, and in a roundabout way, we could suppose that to be true. But, I truly believe the adversary here is referring to the bigger enemy of the "self life." The cry here is for **vengeance** uttered from a **helpless** widow. This widow knew but one thing about her condition and that was the fact that only the **judge** could do anything for her. It's very possible that right here in this parable, we can see Jesus giving us a prophetic look at Pentecost. He knew that once He ascended back to the Father, there would come forth a sound of supplication that would soon follow him into the sweet chambers of the Most High.

That mournful masterpiece ascending from those one hundred twenty broken spirits, would be the anthem for vengeance against mankind's staunchest adversary, our weak and fettered nature! We may be able to see a small clue to confirm this thought in verse seven with the statement, "He will avenge them **SPEEDILY**." This verse appears uncannily close to a familiar verse in Acts chapter two:

> "And **SUDDENLY** there came a sound from heaven as of a rushing mighty wind, and it filled all the house where they were sitting." (Acts 2:2)

The disciples knew the very same thing that the widow in the parable emphatically knew. They were well aware of the task that lay before them and the difficult mandate which their master had given them. "Go ye into all the world and preach" (see Mark 16:15) was far too heavy an order for these folks in their carnal condition. There had to be an appeal within the courts of heaven and a cry to "Avenge us of our adversary." It would need to be a cry that would come up before God from their grounded human insufficiencies. Since the enemies of their souls were just too strong for them, the judge of all the earth would need to act and hand down a verdict of victory to their insufficient souls.

I believe we can also get a clue from verse one as to just what the Master wished to convey:

> "And He spake a parable unto them *to this end*, that men ought always to pray, and not to faint." (Luke 18:1)

It becomes evident by this verse that this parable is clearly speaking about prevailing under the stress of praying. However, it is far from merely praying for relief of our **temporal position** in this world. Nor is He warning about holding up under the burden of praying for a **better life.** Neither is this a peril of passing out from praying for a cool, calm, or collective world to unfold in **our future.** No! This is the prayer of vengeance that goes something like this, "Oh God, we have been defeated too long by the adversary of this limited flesh. With Paul we cry, 'Who will deliver us from this body of death?' (see Romans 7:24). Will you not avenge us speedily, suddenly, without any more delay?!" Oh beloved, when the cry gets just like that, the battalions of righteousness are just over the hills, "Lift up thine eyes from whence cometh thine help!" (see Psalms 121:1).

Consider Acts chapter 2:1 with regards to unity:

> "And when the day of Pentecost was fully come, they were all with **one accord** in one place." (Acts chapter 2:1)

Oh dear friend, consider the scene! A destitute band of rogue Jews who were following a man who had slipped up into the very clouds before them. A man who had left them with a tremendous commission, alongside a tremendous promise, yet, not one without a cost. But firstly, there was a recognition that had to take place among them. This discovery would be the ominous reality that the disciples had **NOTHING** within themselves to complete this task. Before them lay the great plains of Canaan land, which to them, was the conquest of all human hearts for the cause of the gospel! Yet, the giants of human limitation also lay obstinately across their path as well.

We imagine that this time and setting would have been a peaceful time of systematic prayer and a layed out format, yet, it was anything but this. Jesus only gave them one word and that word was "***WAIT!***" Oh the thorn in the flesh that this word is! Anything but that! "Lord, have you no concern that we perish? Can you not act in a more swift manner? Do you not see the beasts of religion encompassing us? Do you not hear the anthem of the wounded consciences of the temple hierarchy? 'Crucify them, crucify them!'"

No beloved, this was not the Sunday morning prayers of a people pampering preacher! Nor was it a mama's plea to get Junior out of jail after he drove his vehicle, while intoxicated, into the local restaurant wall. These pleas were far from petitions of personal preference, this was something divinely desperate! "Avenge us of our adversary!" This vengeance is directed at the very essence of sin within us, as well the sin within all of those who would hear the voice of the beckoning Holy Spirit down through the ages. Oh, that we would have the same simple plea, that we would utter the same cry! Oh God, step down! The enemies of our soul are simply too strong for us.

May we gather together under the mighty trees of righteousness and call out to God that He would plant us as such, within the rich soil of His truth and love. Let this, and this alone, be our unifying cry. Then, will He avenge us indeed, and that right speedily!

> "Behold, how good and how pleasant *it is* for brethren to dwell together in unity!" (Psalm 133:1)

Chapter 5

# A COLD HARD TRUTH

*"Thus saith the LORD, Stand ye in the ways, and see, and ask for the old paths, where is the good way, and walk therein, and ye shall find rest for your souls. But they said, We will not walk therein." Jeremiah 6:16*

IN ORDER TO SET THE TONE for the idea that I wish to convey in this chapter, I must begin by sharing a couple of personal experiences. One experience was a dream, the other was a direct word from God that I received while awake. I will start with the dream.

To this day it still appears just as real as when I experienced it several years ago. In the dream, my wife and I found ourselves in the entrance of a very large city. It appeared to be a city such as New York, or some other metropolitan area. As the gate swung open, we found ourselves just inside the entrance of the city. There was debris flying everywhere, fires in trash cans, cars that had been burned out and buildings with the windows busted out. It was sort of a feeling of a post-apocalypse scenario.

Suddenly, I noticed to my left a man lying on a park bench. This bench was like one of those concrete slabs you see on a couple pedestals in a park and I would realize later that this setting represented sort of like a "slab" in a morgue. The emphasis of this scene was obviously on **death,** as I found myself hovering above the victim lying on this slab. Due to his discoloration and deteriorating condition, this man had obviously been dead for some time. My wife was standing behind me, egging me on and trying feverishly to get me to resuscitate the fellow. As I was just getting ready to give him mouth to mouth resuscitation, suddenly, I heard a voice as if it came from everywhere. This voice sounded, no doubt, like the one that the apostle John heard, which sounded like the voice of many waters. The voice made this declaration in a very authoritative tone:

**"He has been dead too long, you cannot resuscitate him!!!"**

It startled me beyond imagination as I looked around to try and find the source of the voice which was entirely atmospheric and could not be pinned down to a location. I backed out of my attempt at trying to save the man's life, knowing that this voice was the voice of God, and that my feeble efforts to resuscitate that dead carcass was futile. I then immediately woke up from the dream, of course, very shaken.

I pondered the dream for the next few days. Then, while in prayer one morning, the Lord began to unfold the meaning to me. This is how He interpreted it to me. The carcass of the man represented the false doctrinal foundation of the modern church that we have been building upon. My attempts to resuscitate the man, represented my own efforts to find something in the modern church that was **salvageable** in which to **build upon**. This old model is something that cannot be resuscitated, it must be done away with and a new wine skin provided. The surrounding chaos represented the state of the world, which was a subsequent result of the condition of the dead church system.

This experience caused me to realize that my attempts to find something that could be resuscitated within the doctrines of man, were in vain. Any life that was present in the man previously had obviously been drained from him. The result was the church, lying upon a cold slab, in the midst of a dying world. This dream was no doubt my epiphany. It was then and there that I was faced with the dreadful reality of the true state of the modern church. This was a spiritual turning point in my life and ministry and I will never forget it. I will ever be thankful for that moment of awakening.

The second experience that I had was a direct word spoken to me from the Lord. It wasn't audible, but due to its striking delivery, it might as well have been. At the time of this experience, I had previously moved a couple of states away from my home state and was commuting between cities to work everyday. I would drive the same stretch of highway day after day, and in so doing, would pass a very large elaborate church along the way. I had been to the church, so I knew its doctrine. It was one with the message of "***prosperity***" and "***the blessed life***," and basically, by all rights, a typical modern American church.

One morning, as I was passing by that particular church, just as I had done numerous times, I heard the Holy Spirit speak to me expressly. It was one of the most defining and clarion moments I have ever experienced in hearing the Lord's voice. It came with such convincing power, and at a time when least expected. At the moment it came, I wasn't thinking anything along the lines of that church and quite frankly, anything God related at all. If I recall correctly, my mind was on the task of the day, and purely work related. Then suddenly, out of the blue, I heard this statement:

> "Until you see, that **ALL** that you see, is **NOT MY** gospel, you will never preach **MY** gospel!"

This statement sounded like a gun blast going off next to my spiritual ears. It was like a person firing a shotgun too close to you while neglecting to inform you that they were about to do so. I truly did not know how to digest that statement at that time. Surely, I thought, "this is a message I am to give to someone else?" I mean, after all, *I was preaching* the gospel at the time (so I thought, anyway). Little did I know that this was the sequel to the rude awakening I had received in the dream which I previously mentioned. God was trying to get something through the layers of **religion** that had calloused over my unsuspecting heart, and I was not quite sure what that something was.

Over the next few months I continued to digest the statement the Lord had spoken to me that day. Simultaneously, I continued the pursuit of finding a church that I felt was on the move, at least in some capacity, towards the fullness of God. Disappointment after disappointment met me at the door as I began to see a pattern of complacency among pulpit and pew that was increasingly alarming to my soul. I had visited upwards of 40 churches during my pilgrimage, in search of soul hunger, but found precious little. I began to ask in my own heart, more and more, these seemingly unanswerable questions: "Where is the desire for revival? Doesn't anyone see that there is so much more of God that we need to chase after? Do we not see that this current condition of spiritual anemia has no sure path of the life of Christ in it? Is anybody truly awake? Is this truly the way the church is to finish out the age?"

These considerations began to roll over and over in me, all the while blending with those previous two revelations that I had received about the church's condition. A new reality was dawning in my heart. I was now staring at a cold hard truth, straight in the face. That truth is the fact that the modern church, by and large, is dead.

After an exhausting search that had worn myself and my wife completely thin, I finally caught a break. One day I was driving in a part of town that I wasn't familiar with when I passed a small white country church. This road connected two parts of the city and was somewhat more sparse than the other roads around the area. This little church sat pretty much by itself and really looked a bit unused. Again, I heard that same wonderful voice of His Spirit, "That's the one right there." Oh, how often we find that when we have exhausted all our resources, the Lord can then move us into position.

When I got home that evening I embraced my wife and told her, "The Lord spoke to me today, and honey, I've found the one." After rolling her eyes, she expressed her typical disdain at my continual and relentless pilgrimage within the miry clay of the modern church scene. The following Sunday, I made the journey some 30 miles to the city in order to attend the church. My dear wife had at this point given up the attempts and turned the mission of "church tracking" solely over to my discretion. I'm sure I appeared to her as a relentless beagle on an old rabbit trail that had long grown cold.

Days before, when I heard the Lord say this particular church was the right one, I had pulled in to check for the service times. The sign on the front was hanging by one chain, and did not have a time written on it anywhere. I arrived at the church a bit late since I wasn't sure of their starting time. I had taken a guess at the time that it would likely start, but ended up missing it by about a half an hour. When I opened the door and went into the vestibule, I could hear that the fellow was already preaching. I slipped in unassumingly and sat down on the back pew.

When I started to listen to the dear man, my ears perked up. Could it be? Can I truly be hearing this? Had I finally found the old sound of Zion roaring in the sanctuary? Indeed I had, and it was an unimaginable relief to my soul's longing for truth! This would begin a two and a half year relationship that would purge my soul of the many years of false doctrines I had consumed. Systematically, brick by brick, the teaching gift that manifested in this dear brother would re-establish my foundation in the true gospel message of "Repentance from dead works, and faith towards God" (see Hebrews 6:1). I am ever thankful for the Lord's guidance to join with that faithful man. I can say without fear of contradiction that this book could in no way be possible without that brother's obedience to God. Many of the truths I am conveying to you in this book, were either enhanced, confirmed, or revealed through the channel of that teaching gift in that brother.

Let me just say this right here. It's obvious by this story that there are no doubt small pockets of hungry seekers scattered about this country. These belong to the remnant in which God always extracts from the entire fabric of the religious system. These are they who have a spirit of discontent within them. No, they can never be satisfied with the religion of mediocrity. It is not enough for them to push open a Sunday morning double door, shake hands with the system, and cozy down in a favorite pew designated and tailored to their status as a parishioner. Oh, they may very well be sitting in a pew somewhere, but their insides are being eaten up with the reality of their own discontent.

While everything appears fair, chiseled, and finely tuned to a spiritual asceticism all around them, they know better. They have been to the secret place with God and they have heard the call to "Come up hither, and I will shew thee things which will be hereafter" (see Revelation 4:1). They are plagued with the gnawing thought always, there's more, there's more, there's more! It never leaves them, it is carved in their soul by the very sword of the Spirit. I will speak a great deal more upon the subject of this "remnant of the discontent" in a later chapter.

When the Lord Jesus came to this earth, He was facing a dead world, with a cold, dead religion in its midst. He knew that the task that lay ahead was to revisit the foundations of God's purpose for man and renew the full purpose of the law in the earth. Moses' initial visit had failed to produce this reconciliation of God and man, due to the contrary effects of the law upon the rebellious creature. So the mission of Jesus Christ was to revitalize the foundation, and bring it back to a pure, true repentance of the heart, and not just the performance of religion. The cross of Jesus Christ was going to stop the mouth of all religion, declare man guilty before God, and show him his need of emancipation from, not just the **acts of sin**, but the nature of **sin itself.**

This is precisely what the Lord Jesus brought the disciples through while doing away with the old wine skin (the old way of thinking) and providing a new one. It would be a vessel that would not burst with the volatility of the new life that it was about to receive. Likewise, we cannot assume that within the current model of the modern church, we are going to be able to build on these weak and beggarly conditions. The foundations that currently hold her up will collapse under the pressure and give way to the weightiness of the glory of God. The foundation of repentance must be fully revisited, since it is the only thing that can sustain the glory of God. It is when man comes to nothing and acknowledges his utter depravity before a holy God, that He can then take up their case and begin with something anew.

God can never build upon the condition of man, nor is He out to make man a better, more fitting specimen. He does not incrementally **work** on our depraved nature, instead, He brings it to a **death** to itself. He makes man a **new creature** and starts from scratch with an "infant spirit," one that is clean and undefiled. He cannot redo that which has already been marred, this is why man must be **born anew.**

The modern church insidiously teaches that God is somehow **forming you** into a better person **over time.** I call this "Developmental Christianity" and it is simply not the teaching of the Bible, but the teaching of humanism that has insidiously crept into the house of God. Man will never be anything better than what he is, he simply cannot be improved upon. This is why the gospel brings us into the union of Christ's death, so that our old man, the one who's foundation is built upon self-interest, can be put to death **with Him**. This is why the old man in us must be slain (so to speak) and be buried with Christ in baptism (into death) and risen again in the newness of life.

"He's still working on me" is one of the old sayings of Zion, however, it's incredibly theologically incorrect. We have nothing within ourselves to work with, all must be put to death. This is why Peter would call us "Lively stones, are built up a spiritual house" (see 1 Peter 2:5). Our old foundation of self-works is a dwelling place which is dilapidated, uninhabitable, and utterly condemned. It is the nature and virtue of Christ that springs forth and gives us new life and hence becomes a lovely cohabitation of God's Spirit with our spirit. This is what it means to be conformed to the image of Christ. This has nothing to do with God **working** a piece of clay and trying to fashion it into a lovely piece of **artwork.** It simply means when God has poured His Spirit into our life, our spirit will take on the very nature of Christ. It is our earthly vessel that must be brought under the subjection of this new life. The body must now be brought under the subjection of the bidding and virtues of the Spirit of Christ.

It is "Christ in us" that is the hope of glory. Meaning, that it is the very indwelling Spirit that glorifies Christ in the **inner man.** That Glory is shared with us through His Spirit and that is what we **conform to** (see John 17:22). It is not God trying to **reform** us, it is us being **conformed** to God, through a voluntary yielding of our members to that influence that is now within us. This is why it is called **regeneration**, and not **reformation.** It is done with resurrection power, and not mere willpower. I like to call it "spiritual displacement." It is to be filled with God, and self to be pushed out. As God gains more ground in us, it is a simple yielding forth of the virtues of God. It is not you becoming a **better** person, but simply you becoming more of a **dead** person, one who gets out of the way of the new man. This alone gives way to the life of Christ within.

The modern church often attempts to call the work of sanctification, which is simply "to be set apart by cleansing," a "***process.***" This to me, has almost a ***factory*** sound to it. I would rather, like Paul, see it as a ***reckoning.*** "Likewise reckon (decide or reason) ye also yourselves to be dead indeed unto sin, but alive unto God through Jesus Christ our Lord" (Romans 6:11). If we call the cleansing work of God in the soul a ***process,*** this almost inevitably implies an incremental work of man's own systematic ***timing*** in dealing with his own sin (at his own discretion). It in essence gives man the ***right*** to move at his own pace, rolling off of the assembly line of self-improvement, a product of his own making.

I have often made this statement: Sanctification is not a ***process***, as much as it is a ***person.*** "But of Him are ye in Christ Jesus, who of God is ***made unto us*** wisdom, and righteousness, and ***sanctification***, and redemption" (1 Corinthians 1:30). The infilling of God's Spirit is ever moving to fullness within us. This ***reckoning*** of death to ourselves and to sin, must be induced, motivated, and implemented by the Spirit of Christ within us. Sanctification is the simple decision to yield ourselves to the loving influence of the Spirit of God, and give way to His movings in our heart. It is man's cooperation with the divine intent of God to set His creature apart for the privilege of the use of his Creator. "For this is the will of God, even your sanctification" (see 1 Thessalonians 4:3). This alone can cleanse, this alone can keep one, and this alone can equip one for service.

Paul also declares, "Yield your members as servants of righteousness" (see Romans 6:13). This is the only way the gospel works. We could try and swallow an entire camel, but we still will not be able to strain out one gnat of righteousness. "I am crucified with Christ, nevertheless I live, yet not I, but Christ liveth in me" (see Galatians 2:20). This verse must become an actual reality in the believer's life, there is simply no other way to true victory.

Let us fast forward a couple thousand years from the time of Paul's penmanship, to our moment in time. We must truly make a comparative analysis and consider the spiritual condition of things. Regardless of the constant clamoring of the positive thinkers and motivational zealots, the religious system is once again in a man-made hole. The following passage in the book of Jeremiah aptly describes our day and age as it did also concerning those to whom it was first written:

> "For my people have committed two evils; they have forsaken me the fountain of living waters, *and* hewed them out cisterns, broken cisterns, that can hold no water." (Jeremiah 2:13)

The modern church has become a holding tank for all things man-made. She has excavated deeply into the mountainside of humanistic philosophy for the betterment of man's comfort. There, she has been able to store up the waters of her own making, and in the name of self-sustenance, been able to eke out enough moisture to somehow survive. Nevertheless, this indictment from God to the children of Israel, would ring with the same truth inside the hallowed halls of our most sacred religious institutions.

These "two evils" could easily be pronounced upon the modern church without fear of contradiction or a bonafide pushback. Insidiously over time, she has drifted away from her fundamental roots. Not long ago in her not too distant past, she was dependent on the movements of God's Spirit (***the fountain***). This divine source is the direct effect upon our human condition through conviction of sin and righteousness. Conversely, she has now opted to fill her pews with the coaxing methods of an intellectual approach from (***the cisterns***). These are but man-made methodologies that make fleshly appeals to the mind.

The gospel has been systematically dressed down, and formed into the "cool guy" that everyone wants at the party. "Another Jesus" has now emerged who is social, relevant, and noninvasive to our lifestyles. This ***Jesus*** is a made to order "form of godliness" (see 2 Timothy 3:5) version, that loves pleasure, has your best interests in mind, and rides along in your train of destiny to watch the vulnerable tracks ahead. No longer do we preach the true message of the cross which promotes the loss of **YOUR** life for the gospel, and **SUBMISSION** to the **LORDSHIP** of Jesus.

Oh beloved! Let us fill in the cisterns of modern thinking with the dirt of true doctrinal power! Let us find our shovels of conviction and bury the useless methods of humanistic appeal far beneath the ground! May we grab our picks and dig till we rediscover that grown over fountain of God! Let us search our hearts again and find that old river, springing up into everlasting life! Oh how we need to cry out to God to bring it forth again from our very bellies! Ask for the old paths and He will bring it to pass!

> Spring up O well, within my soul,
> Spring up O well, and make me whole,
> Spring up O well, and give to me
> That life, abundantly!
> (Source: hymn by Mary A. Lathbury)

Chapter 6

# POSITION OR POSSESSION?

*"Examine yourselves, whether ye be in the faith; prove your own selves. Know ye not your own selves, how that Jesus Christ is in you, except ye be reprobates?"* 2 Corinthians 13:5

ONE OF THE MOST DISTURBING CONDITIONS of the modern church is its "Christless conversions." If you were to conduct a poll and launch an investigation of its patrons, you would find that within its walls are no want of **professors of faith.** Conversely, you would be hard pressed to find many **possessors of Christ Himself.** What a difference a couple of letters can make in a word! In the above passage in 2 Corinthians, we see the distinction that Paul wishes to draw between being a mere professor of religion, and a possessor of Christ. Although these words are very close in spelling, they are as far different as the north pole is from the south in meaning. I think that here at this juncture, it would do us justice to call upon the Greek definition for a closer look at the word reprobate as it is demonstrated in our opening verse.

> Derived from the word : adokimos- ***not standing the test, not approved***; properly of metals and coins. (Source: Thayer's Greek Lexicon)

As we can see within the definition of reprobate, this word implies a failure of some kind, "A coming up short," so to speak. As a past dealer of precious metals (ie. gold, silver, platinum) I can attest to this testing procedure first hand. In the modern vernacular, we call it "the acid test" and it has to do with the reaction of metals to acid being applied to it. If the metal we were dealing with, whether coinage or jewelry, was ever in question due to being unclearly stamped or suspect in coloration, it was then subjected to the scrutiny of nitric acid. A small area of the item would be ground off, or filed, in order to breach the surface of the material. By doing so, it would afford a place for the acid to be applied. When the acid hit the exposed metal it would react according to the percentage of the precious metal within its composition.

With gold, for instance, it would vary in volatility and color which would thereby determine what karat (percentage of gold) it contained (ie. 10K,14K,18K). If it contained no gold, it would simply bubble violently and turn an almost neon green. Based upon this volatile reaction from the acid, it could be immediately determined whether or not the metal's interior content was precious or not. If it was simply **plated** on the exterior with surface gold (in order to **appear** real), the acid would expose its true internal substance by its volatile effect on it. However, if we were to test 24 karat gold, the outcome would be far different. Due to the utter purity that it had gained through **refinement**, it would show zero effects from the acid.

So in light of that example, let us consider what a true reprobate is: To be a **reprobate** simply means that the true acid test of spirituality cannot be passed due to the wrong substance making up the **inside** of a thing, nothing more, nothing less. It literally means **one who is void of the inner Christ** and one who does not possess the nature and virtues of a living God within their heart. This self-examination that Paul here pushes, is to test this personal thesis in every soul, "Does Christ truly abide within?" It must be noted here that this word in no way implies an "***eternal loss,***" as much of the modern church has so taught it, but merely an ***insufficient condition*** of the heart. It in no way suggests that such a person is unredeemable, but simply that they are lost (shipwrecked), and in need of the indwelling Savior.

When the acid of this world's volatile nature is poured mercilessly upon the saint and the sinner alike, the test will be clear. He who has the faith and virtues **OF** the Son of God within, will be able to absorb all evil without retaliation, or retribution, just as their master did. If Christ is ***NOT*** in His temple (the human spirit) then they will not be able to repel all such evil, but will instead draw the sword of personal valor and vindicate their own reputation. This is the true test of Christianity and the patience of the saints being evident (see Revelation 14:12). Satan's persecution and constant buffering of the church is the "nitric acid," placed upon the 24 karat gold of the very "faith of the Son of God" within us. "I counsel thee to buy of me, ***gold*** tried in the fire" (see Revelation 3:18). This ***gold*** is no doubt the very nature of the Lord Jesus and His unswerving faith and virtues that we must have within our own heart.

Multitudes today have been peddled a cheap novelty version of the gospel which has only been presented to the intellect, yet, not touching the heart. It is a "plated gospel" and one of topical asceticism. It is much like that ***cheaper*** costume jewelry that has merely been covered with an overlay of ***surface gold***, while yet remaining useless metal within. It is a gospel of mental assent, a form of godliness that supplies zero power to emancipate from sin. Millions have been lured to sleep by an easy-believism that requires no cross bearing, nor crucifixion of the old life. It is a drive-thru salvation and an "order at the speaker, pick up at the window" kind of appeal.

This modern, mystical, metaphorical version of salvation has become a matter of ***position*** rather than a matter of ***possession.*** The misled masses are herded like cattle by religious rustlers into the branding corrals. Here, they are administered a brand of ownership that is only burnt into the surface of the "foreskin of their hearts." On the contrary, God calls on us to "Circumcise therefore the foreskin of your heart, and be no more stiff-necked" (see Deuteronomy 10:16). Unfortunately for the recipients of this topical treatment, this deception runs much deeper than an exterior branding mark. It is rather the searing of the most precious possession of the human condition, the conscience. When a dear soul is led blindly down the **Romans Road** (the sinner's prayer) without coming through the terrors of Mt. Sinai (conviction by the law), they are errantly prescribed a topical ointment in order to treat a more deep set infirmity. If a soul does not experience the convincing power of the Holy Ghost in order to show them their sin, they cannot know the need for the liberation of such. Allow me to explain.

The law came sizzling down on Sinai to show the terrible contrast between a holy God and a grossly disobedient creature (i.e. mankind). Without this contrast being clearly drawn, the creature could have never seen the mercy that was necessary to forgive it, and to liberate it from its unholy impotence. In other words, the law of God is the awakening rod to the unruly child of iniquity within all of us. It was there on Sinai, that God disclosed His holy nature and His demands of conformity to such. When the Mount shook and both Moses and the people "did exceedingly shake and tremble," this daunting display was to make sin, utterly sinful.

Now, fast forward a few hundred years to the time of Jesus' arrival and what do we find? A forthright John the Baptist standing on a river bank heralding spiritual declarations of a divine tree cutting to all of

Judea. This fanatical forerunner, bearing the ax of transition, would point to a baptiser. No, not a baptiser in water, but a baptiser of fire! That camel hair covered prophet would indict the entire religious hierarchy with the searing law of God. This fiery brand of preaching would even bring the whole community down to the water's edge, saying, "And what shall we do?" (see Luke 3:14). He indeed had an ax to grind, and that implement in his hand was for the chopping down of the heretofore useless religious system. This piety of pretense had enslaved humankind with the mountainous mendacities of rules and regulations!

The word of God and the call to repentance emitting from John would replicate that sound on the mountain several hundred years before, when Moses tossed those sacred stones down in front of the frivolous congregation of Israel. The Lord knows His business in winning humanity. He knows He must first establish the great divide between the divine and the carnal by blowing the trumpet blast of His searing law upon the ears of the spiritually complacent. This was the testimony of the man of God when describing the molten mountain experience!

> "And so terrible was the sight, *that* Moses said, I exceedingly fear and quake." (see Hebrews 12:21)

We must revisit the Sinai experience in our modern preaching. The nature of God must be elevated and His **otherness** be clearly seen through the declaration of His law. Righteousness preaching has gone by the wayside and has given way to a self-seeking, palatial pampering of magnanimous proportions. The pulpit must return to the "***cleft of the rock***" and await the "***passing by***" of this glorious God! If only we can catch but a glimpse of the hinder parts of the Lord, that glory would then translate to the masses.

John the Baptist, like Moses, had a mission specific. It would be to prepare the way of the Lord and to make straight paths for **His** feet. This is no doubt the declaration of God's blessed holy nature to a spiritually slumbering humanity. It is what brings mankind to the river bank of decision and the awakening of his dead conscience. If man does not see the great contrast between God's lofty divinity, and his satanically driven decadence within his own bosom, he cannot possibly see his need for a Savior. The need for conviction is beyond paramount to the true conversion of the sinner, without it, it is as an attempt to use an ointment upon leprosy.

Suppose a doctor calls upon a person that has no symptoms. This individual has received no diagnosis of being terminally ill, yet the doctor immediately and carelessly prescribes a plethora of medicines to treat all manners of inner diseases. Would the public not cry ***quack*** at such an oversight and such a dangerous presumption? Indeed, we would see it as nothing but a most grievous violation of the Hippocratic Oath. The doctor would be called in front of the great medical board and indicted with gross malpractice. Now, consider this same way of thinking in regards to spiritual treatment. If we are only presenting the cross of Jesus Christ as a ***remedy***, without the knowledge of the inner ***disease of sin***, then we are also guilty of gross spiritual malpractice.

So, what is the end result of such empty preaching that is void of the convincing power of the Holy Ghost? It can be nothing but a ***topical*** conversion which will only produce a salvation of the head, and not a salvation of the heart. If Christ ceases to enter His temple (our body) through true broken repentance, then He only abides in the outer courts of the soul. He stands without, knocking upon the door of the sacred place of the inner chambers of the heart. He may only be **WITH** you, but He seeks to be **IN** you (see John 14:17).

## POSITION OR POSSESSION?

These questions still remain to all those who would call themselves His: Is Christ in His temple? Is His nature there, is His righteousness manifesting in the bosom? Has the satanic nature been put down? Has there been a one hundred eighty degree turn? Is there truly a new man there? Let us be candid, let us be searchable, let us be transparent, let us be willing to come under that great examination light of the piercing eyes of "Him who is invisible" (see Hebrews 11:27). May we take the great test and see, is Jesus Christ within, or without? It is the only true test that matters.

Let us end this chapter with the resounding truth of the word of God, spoken through our wonderfully separated apostle to the Gentiles:

> "But ye are not in the flesh, but in the Spirit, if so be that the Spirit of God dwell in you. Now if any man have not the Spirit of Christ, he is none of His." (Romans 8:9)

Chapter 7

# A MESSAGE TO MINISTERS

*"Woe be unto the pastors that destroy and scatter the sheep of my pasture! saith the LORD." Jeremiah 23:1*

THIS BOOK WOULD BE dreadfully incomplete without a section that addresses the problem of the pulpit. In the next few chapters, I will attempt to break down this ominous 23rd chapter of Jeremiah and apply it to our times, as it may fit. We will likewise delve into the book of 1st Samuel to place an emphatic exclamation point on this matter of the clergy. In this 23rd chapter of Jeremiah we see probably the most scorching rebuke directed at the Lord's earthly representatives in the entire book of God. This torching treatise of rabbinical rebuke starts with the words **WOE**! No word describes better this divine lamentation of the Lord over His broken and battered sheepfold, due to the neglect of His shepherds. It's almost as if He must declare: "Oh, I must now expose my overseers! They are not responding to my prophet's rebuke, and now I am forced to act! Let us take the covers off of this tragedy of spiritual adultery and allow the whole universe to observe!"

Let us feel the thunder in our souls of this opening rebuke from this holy God!

"Woe be unto the pastors that destroy and scatter the sheep of my pasture! saith the LORD." (Jeremiah 23:1)

Continuing to the second verse, we see just who this indictment is handed down to:

"Therefore, thus saith the LORD God of Israel against the pastors that **FEED** my people; Ye have scattered my flock, and driven them away, and have not visited them: behold, I will visit upon you the evil of your doings, saith the LORD." (Jeremiah 23:2)

It becomes apparent here that Jeremiah is not speaking of pastors that have completely ***abandoned*** the flock. Rather, He chastises those who are ***still feeding*** the flock, yet all the while, failing to nurture them. Also, let us note that a "scattering" of the flock is mentioned here. Basically, these disconnected shepherds were being depicted as those who do in fact tread out the grain. However, they apathetically walk away from the feeding bins with no concern as to whether the food is being properly digested or shared. It becomes very clear that a cohesive element had been lost at the feeding troughs of God's word. In other words, the feed was still being spread about for the flocks, yet the ***kind*** and ***quality*** of the feed is where the blame must surely be laid. The scolding of the Lord concerning this scattering and the lack of proper feed, would attest to the fact that the shepherds had gotten their eyes off the health and unity of the sheep. Yes, they were ***still*** feeding, but their lack-luster view of the Divine had spilled over into the feeding bins and had become mingled with the grains of utter complacency. These pastors were inadvertently driving away the flock by the default of a ***poor diet.***

Sheep will never be able to stay where they cannot be properly fed, they will either perish with hunger, or at best, suffer from gross malnutrition. If given the option, they will always saunter away to greener pastures by default of their very own survival instincts. In the modern vernacular we call this "church hopping," or "church shopping," and it is indicative of one of two things. It is either due to the fact that those pasture hopping individuals are not receiving the nutrients necessary to their spiritual advancement, or, they are the kind of sheep that are but "heaping to themselves" (see 2 Timothy 4:3) a more palpable message of leisure. Although the "easy-believism" crowds are growing exponentially, we cannot assume that it is always the latter of the two that causes this continual exodus. I personally believe that in the modern era, it is far too easy to dismiss and to assume that this class of jittery, wandering sheep, are simply the unpleasant fold of the forever discontented. Nay, but to the contrary, many are simply fed up with the food and are feeling the malnourishment of such a dainty nutritional portion.

It is far easier for the man of God to look in the mirror and see no evil and therefore blame the wandering sheep. It is much more difficult to self-indict and to lay before a holy God in a humble breaking of spiritual bankruptcy! Oh! Let us see some bankrupt preachers! Give us some who would say in transparent soul searching honesty, "I have not adequate food for the flocks! Rend the heavens and come down oh God, I confess my void and the fact that without you, I can do **NOTHING**! I toss away from my person all the books of higher learning and exegetical janglings and call upon a God who answers by fire! Consume me oh Most High with the zeal of thine kingdom! Allow me to feel the divine heartbeat and eternal passion for your sheep, oh God!"

Have you cried thusly man of God? If you have not, I would pray that you do so quickly so that thy **lampstand will not be taken!** I pray that this has not already happened to you, dear shepherd.

As we scan through this chapter in Jeremiah, we see a great theme unfolding. That theme is that God always cares for the flock, even when it has gone astray under the hands of careless clergymen. This is where it gets *dicey* for the man of God. The Lord's desire is to always get to the hungry flock at any cost, even to the point of dealing with the overseers who are the obstructions between Him and the apple of His eye. In the 3rd and 4th verse we see the remedy coming forth:

> "And I will gather the remnant of my flock out of all countries whither I have driven them, and will bring them again to their folds; and they shall be fruitful and increase. And I will **set up shepherds** over them which **shall feed them**: and they shall fear no more, nor be dismayed, neither shall they be lacking, saith the LORD." (Jeremiah 23: 3-4)

So here we see that God has a plan to rescue the lost and emaciated lambs that have wandered off due to a lack of care. This "remnant" has always been His way of bringing alive again His ideal in the earth. His personal care and nourishment is played out in this scenario of the gathering of the weak, rejected, and overburdened flocks. In so gathering them, He then outfits them with overseers that spring forth from His own heart of compassion for them. These benevolent bishops are put in place by God to eliminate *fear* (from predators), *dismay* (from trauma), and *lack* (from insufficient nourishment), within that flock. Man of God, you must know this: the Lord will certainly feed His flocks who are hungry and cry to Him for truth. Consequently, He will move out of the way, whom He needs to move out of the way, in order to do so.

The worst thing (or the best thing if he joins them) that can happen to a pastor or overseer is that the sheep would cry out for truth. When this cry ascends into the ears of God, it triggers His wonderful compassion for His wayfaring lambs. The pastor over such a flock who is failing to feed such clamoring palates, will find himself in a very precarious place. He will then be the subject of Holy Ghost scrutiny and come under the radar of the searching, fiery eyes, of one called the Alpha and Omega. One who "Searches the hearts and tries the reins" (see Jeremiah 17:10), to give every man according to his deeds. If he is weighed in the balance and found wanting, the Lord will then begin the process of **conviction of his condition**, or the **eviction of his position**. One of these two responses will be handed down from the Lord, and this, of course, is contingent upon the openness, or the rebellion of the man's heart. Dear man of God, please hear this admonition. Please do not be an obstruction when the people of God begin to cry out, but instead, humble yourself and get thy face upon the ground and cry out alongside!

In the third chapter of Revelation we have an account of the Lord Jesus Christ coming with great passion and concern to a tepid church. This particular assembly is admonished over its lack of zeal and its "ho hum" complacency. This "unbridled bride" has spots on her wedding dress that even she herself was not aware of. Her eyes had crusted over with the sands of complacency and had matted shut, causing her great blindness. She was badly in need of the discerning salve of truth to be rubbed on her eyelids once again, "that she mayest see" the true state of her condition. As the Lord deals out these indictments of truth to her lukewarm condition, He informs her that she is under the false presumption of having been *increased* with goods and, consequently, in need of nothing. But the Lord has divine eyesight and sees her instead to be wretched, miserable, and poor, blind, and naked. These "**goods**

***that had increased*** " were no doubt her own works, manifested out of her own resources, that made void the need for God's influence in the assembly.

We must keep in mind that these seven letters to seven different churches were written to the "***angels***" of the churches. Some here may make the argument that these letters are being delivered to angelic overseers that are assigned to each assembly. However, the word ***angel*** here could hold a duality of meanings and depending on the context, It could either be speaking of a celestial being, or a human being. It is simply referring to a ***delegate, representative, or a messenger,*** and not ***necessarily*** of a divine source alone. In other words, it is simply one who speaks on the behalf of God, to man. It would make no sense to me for an apostle to deliver words ***from*** Jesus ***to*** celestial beings, and then back to the churches, as this would be contradictory to all other revealed biblical accounts.

Imagine being a minister of a local parish and opening your church mailbox. In it, you find a letter marked "From the third heavens," and addressed directly to you! You open the envelope with trembling hands and find the contents to be a fiery treatise on the state of your very own congregation. As you read the list of charges brought against the assembly, beads of sweat begin to form on your forehead and a slight tremor begins in your legs. Your eyes fall towards the bottom of the page and stop abruptly on the ominous words:

> "As many as I love, I rebuke and chasten: be zealous therefore, and repent. Behold, I stand at the door, and knock: if any man hear my voice, and open the door, I will come in to him, and will sup with him, and he with me." (Revelation 3:19-20)

Suddenly, you realize the reality of what is truly before you! It is a warning **directly** from the Son of God, to you, personally! You quickly awaken to the fact that nothing is hidden after all, and that all things are "Open to Him with whom we have to do" (see Hebrews 4:13). You picture in your mind the Lord Jesus Himself, knocking on your parsonage door with great earnestness, inquiring to have an interview with you regarding your status as an overseer. Outside, you hear the voice of many waters entreating. "Behold, I stand at the door and knock oh man of God! I wish to dine with my sheep in intimate fellowship of the breaking of my bread, and the pouring out of my wine. Be zealous therefore and repent of being the obstacle between myself and my people! Open the door oh man of God, let me walk among my golden candlesticks."

I ask you dear minister, could such a letter apply to you? Have you allowed your congregation to settle down into the mundane rut of mediocrity? Have they but entered into a "Form of godliness, denying the power thereof"? (see 2 Timothy 3:5). The Lord is knocking, entreating thee to open! You are the doorkeeper, you are the **one** who "can hear His voice and open the door." Remember, **you are** the angel, and the letter **IS to you**! Your hand is on the inside of the knob, while His knuckles wrap upon the exterior of the door. What's it going to be, dear overseer, shall He enter or no? Or, will you tell Him to go away since you are managing things just fine without Him.

Oh the gravity of this! May all the clergy enter into this ominous revelation of the passion of Jesus for His sheep. How badly He longs for intimate communion with those wayfaring lambs! Those who have been starved out by the rations of religious rituals and deprived by the default of formalism. Oh, do hear it preacher! Open the door and let the Lord at His lambs!

"I counsel thee to buy of me gold tried in the fire, that thou mayest be rich; and white raiment, that thou mayest be clothed, and *that* the shame of thy nakedness do not appear; and anoint thine eyes with eyesalve, that thou mayest see." (Revelation 3:18)

"He that hath an ear, let him hear what the Spirit saith unto the churches. (Revelation 3:22)

In the proceeding chapter, we will explore the life of just such a man who failed to open the door. No, it is not a man who heeded God's warning, but rather one who let his earthly connections and familial favorings trump the importance of the high office. Let us continue the narrative with his example.

# Chapter 8

# THE CHANGING OF THE GUARDS

*"For promotion cometh neither from the east, nor from the west, nor from the south. But God is the judge: He putteth down one, and setteth up another." Psalm 75:6-7*

IN THE FIRST BOOK OF SAMUEL, we see one of the most frightening accounts in the Bible of God's dealings with a careless clergyman and a frivolous father. The lack of time and space would forbid me to cover all the patterns in this account and their relative application to our times, nevertheless, we will skim the highlights afforded to us in the first few chapters of 1st Samuel.

In this man named Eli we can certainly see a type, at least in many cases, of modern ministers and their waning spiritual eyesight. Israel, at the time of the writing of this book of Samuel, had indeed fallen into a religious rut of unpassionate priesthood. We can almost equate the demeanor of God's representative high position among men, the priesthood, as turning into a "security guard" status at this point in history. Eli had become much like the security guard of the local mall who has been at the same gig for a long period of time. It had become commonplace for him to make his rounds, jiggle some doors to assure they are locked, and scour the joint at closing for any stray hideabouts.

A certain complacency sets in during absence of true excitement, and a natural routine emerges. It is inevitable that when there is no break in the mundane atmosphere of the norm, the heart grows numb. I believe Eli draws a very distinct pattern as to how this unfolds. In the first chapter we have him rebuking the praying patron of Hannah at the altar of prayer as she pleads to her Creator for a manchild to be conceived in her barren womb. The irony of this will later unfold. Allow us to observe the account in this particular collection of verses:

> "And it came to pass, as she continued praying before the LORD, that Eli marked her mouth. Now Hannah, she spoke in her heart; only her lips moved, but her voice was not heard: therefore Eli thought she had been drunken. And Eli said unto her, How long wilt thou be drunken? Put away thy wine from thee. And Hannah answered and said, No, my lord, I *am* a woman of a sorrowful spirit: I have drunk neither wine nor strong drink, but have poured out my soul before the LORD. Count not thine handmaid for a daughter of Belial: for out of the abundance of my complaint and grief have I spoken hitherto. Then Eli answered and said, 'Go in peace: and the God of Israel grant *thee* thy petition that thou hast asked of Him.'" (1 Samuel 1:12-17)

Right here we see a couple things of noteworthy mention. It is both a lack of discernment on the part of the priest, and consequently, a religious indictment upon an otherwise gushing fountain of a broken heart. Eli had become so spiritually complacent that he could no longer see the unutterable gushings of a human heart, but instead, attributed them to mere intoxication (Do we have a type of Pentecost here?). To a man who simply wished to cut the lights, grab his briefcase and go home for the night, he perceived this more of an inconvenience than the birthing of a divine dream. Little did he know that in pronouncing that blessing upon her in verse 17, that a manchild of great spiritual zeal would be birthed from that womb. This very child would grow to be the **REPLACEMENT** for the **COMPLACENT**! Even to the point of informing this priest of his own defrocking at a later point in time.

This child yet to be born would also literally bring Israel back from the brink of apostasy, and not to mention, help to usher in her most valiant earthly king to power in her history, in one David. This Samuel, born out of anguish and offered back to the Lord by his grateful mother, would find himself in a most peculiar situation. But, time and space could not afford the pages it would take to praise the faithfulness of a Samuel, we are here rather to observe the complacency of the cleric, even Eli.

Let us continue to the second chapter of Samuel and observe the real tragedy in this account. After Samuel was given over to the Lord by Hannah in order to abide in the temple for service, we are then shown the nature of the problem of that current priesthood. Eli's two sons emerge in this account as two villains bent on the defacing of the Holy sacraments of God. Fittingly, in the 12th verse they earn the title, "*sons of Belial*" (the Devil), yet, these are the priests of the temple of God! They are the very representatives of God to the people! What is this? Satan in the sanctuary? Certainly God would not allow such! Surely this can't be true that Satan's agents have come into the Holy place? Why, certainly someone would have caught this! Surely there must be discernment in the house of God, if no other place on the planet!

At this juncture, let us take the opportunity to make a very important point. The men and women of God, who are in any position which is representative of Him in any capacity of ministerial level, must understand this paramount point. That is the fact that they are the **GATEKEEPERS** of the sanctuary. The Lord once put this thought in my heart while pondering about the many pulpits who refuse to let corrective ministerial rebuke and admonishment in them. Ministers are not only responsible to keep the *bad* stuff away from the sacred wooden podium, but just as guilty are those who refuse to allow *good* corrective admonishment in. Many ministers are simply afraid to have their congregation searched out by the searchlight of truth. This is high spiritual treason and the utmost of tragedies.

Many men of God have unfortunately settled down into a pattern of perceived normalcy and wish not for the apple cart to be toppled. Oftentimes, there is simply too much at stake to take the risk of stirring up such a hornets nest. Perhaps it is a monetary persuasion that becomes the preventer. Maybe it's due to the church mortgage note on their desk that they stare down at monthly. Or, perhaps it is the waning flow of cash that is inadequate to sustain their current operations. These two things may cause them to wince at any hindrance that could be fiscally fatal. Furthermore, there could be positions such as: deacons, board members, larger donors, **WIVES,** within the local body, that when those classes feel threatened, they cause a tumult not easily extinguished.

These dear men have but resigned to be amicable and cooperative, even dare we say, compromising, to avoid such mutiny. Possibly, in their minds, they see everything set on autopilot until they can retire and get out from under the turmoil of being the captain of such an unruly ship. Perhaps they may see the ministry as more of a dynasty of sorts, and feel more comfortable to keep it in the family and hand it down, so to speak. Which, by the way, was the very sin of Eli that we are going to take a hard look at momentarily. In any case, whatever the motivations may be for keeping the prophets at bay and their pulpits clear of rebuke, they are but earthly, sensual, and devilish schemes. These compromises are offered to the man of God by Satan in order to keep the fires of truth to a controllable minimum.

Dear man of God, if you are in such a category, please reconsider this dreadful position! Search out your own heart with God's candle, it is but your own spirit that knows if these things abide within your bosom. Step back, take a good look at yourself in the reflective mirror of the law of liberty, and see if such a blemish appears upon your holy attire. If you see it there, shake yourself. Quickly grab a new garment from the wardrobe of truth, cast off the garment which is spotted by the flesh, and put ye on the garment of righteousness. There is still time to change, there is still time to reverse and your "judgment may yet slumbereth" and the Lord may be granting you space to repent.

As we continue on in this second chapter of 1st Samuel, we see the theme of Eli's great complacency continuing to unfold. Beginning at the 22nd verse we are afforded a glimpse into the tragedy of the particulars of this complacency:

> "Now Eli was very old, and heard all that his sons did unto all Israel; and how they lay with the women that assembled *at* the door of the tabernacle of the congregation. And he said unto them, Why do ye such things? For I hear of your evil dealings by all these people. Nay, my sons; for *it is* no good report that I hear: ye make the LORD'S people to transgress. If one man sin against another, the judge shall judge him: but if a man sin against the LORD, who shall intreat for him? Notwithstanding they hearkened not unto the voice of their father, because the LORD would slay them" (1 Samuel 1:22-25).

We must take notice here of a very telling phrase in the 23rd verse: "For I **hear** of your evil dealings by **ALL THIS PEOPLE**." Here lies the first uncovered aspect of this tragedy! It was the fact that this man of God had to hear the news from the **people** and not from **God** Himself! We must ask these two questions at this juncture: Is the man of God so out of touch with the priesthood that he must rely on the hearsay of the congregation over his own discerning eyes and ears? Or, is this just a case of a father who chose to turn his head until the overwhelming accumulation of iniquity of his sons were too much to sweep under the rug any longer? We know that one of these motivations must have forced him to address his son's iniquities. Only the Lord and Eli himself know which reason was the culprit for such a delay of action. Regardless of the motive, the outcome is still the same. The outcome is that the work of God will suffer, which is the inevitable result of such complacency.

This whole scenario surrounding Eli and his sons presents before us a spiritual principle most alarming, and certainly one that could be easily related to our very own church age in which we live. It is the very avenue by which falsity, compromise, and worldliness creep into the house of God. When we take on a lackadaisical view of sin and treat it as but a casual lion in the bush, it affords the opportunity for its subtle encroachment upon the whole of the flock. This is ultimately how the doctrines of devils have entered the synagogue. In so dealing with sin in a "slight" manner it becomes necessary for us to have a doctrine to match the dilemma, which inevitably unfolds in such an environment. That is, the dichotomy of the **habitation of holiness** and the **synagogue of sin** being able to dwell together in the same temple. This is right where the child of compromise was born.

Satan found that such a babe would surely be received if left upon the doorstep of the floundering church that was barren of true righteousness and could not otherwise produce her own children. This offspring of devils called "unconditional grace" would become the perfect gift for a church wrestling with its own sin and shortcomings. A covering was certainly needed to be able to cope with the onslaught of iniquity in the very house of God.

Although we may make this same kind of inquiring statement such as Eli made concerning his sons: "Why do ye such things?" Nevertheless, our chiding proceeds no further than the question! We feel that in some justifying kind of way, as long as we acknowledge the sins, this is adequate for the appeasement of heaven. Hence, we have transformed the meaning of repentance into a mere statement and **ACKNOWLEDGEMENT OF SIN** and have fallen away from the **FORSAKING OF SIN** side of the definition. We must get back to the understanding of the true gospel. This is a gospel that deals with the *removal* of sin from the heart and not just a *covering up*, due to the simple acknowledgement thereof. The following proverb shows us God's intention in dealing with man and his sin:

> "He that covereth his sins shall not prosper: but whoso confesseth and forsaketh them shall have mercy." (Proverbs 28:13)

Very clearly in this passage we are exposed to a God that literally places a criteria upon mercy! We of course know that God is abundant in mercy, longsuffering, patience, and in love with mankind. However, mercy is not simply peddled out to the mere *confessor* of sin, but rather, only to the willing *forsaker* thereof. Eli's statement to his sons was no doubt one of acknowledgement, yet, all the while entirely void of action. Herein lies the great tragedy of any approach to sin other than one that calls for action concerning its existence in the camp.

Samuels are born in these moments. These conditions of complacency and lack of disdain for depravity, call for such a one to come forth. An Eli environment creates the need for a Samuel response. The difference between these two entities is the obvious, one being that of mere words, and the other being one of action. If the Eli mindset does not turn from its line of thinking, then God will bring the Samuel mentality into existence.

> "And Samuel grew, and the LORD was with him, and did let none of his words fall to the ground." (1 Samuel 3:19)

May we return to the true definition of repentance! A changing of our mind concerning sin and a willingness to forsake it, and not merely a topical confession. If the clergy fail to bring us back to this foundation, a changing of the guards will inevitably be in order!

Lord, give us Eli's who will repent!

And Samuels who are sent!

Chapter 9

# THE TRICKLE DOWN EFFECT

*"Be thou diligent to know the state of thy flocks, and look well to thy herds." Proverbs 27:23*

AS WE RETURN to the 23rd chapter of Jeremiah, we find a most expressive lamentation pouring forth from the weeping prophet. In verses 9 through 11, we get a little glimpse into the severity of Israel's plight while under the influence of an apostate priesthood and profane prophets.

> "Mine heart within me is broken because of the prophets; all my bones shake; I am like a drunken man, and like a man whom wine hath overcome, because of the LORD, and because of the words of His holiness. For the land is full of adulterers; for because of swearing the land mourneth; the pleasant places of the wilderness are dried up, and their course is evil, and their force *is* not right. For both prophet and priest are profane; yea, in my house have I found their wickedness, saith the LORD." (Jeremiah 23:9-11)

Due to the state of the disconnected clergy, we hear in these passages the grieving heart of God transferring through the pen of the prophet. Jeremiah is here seeing in the Spirit this terrible insult to a holy

God and it causes his very bones to shake. This indictment is always handed down firstly to the pulpit and then trickles down to the congregation. Let us look in verse 10 for a closer look at the process of spiritual decay. Here, the prophet starts by mentioning the end result.

> "For the land is full of adulterers; for because of swearing, the land mourneth; the pleasant places of the wilderness are dried up." (Jeremiah 23:10)

The curse of profanity, and the audacity of adultery had so penetrated the normalcy of everyday life that it appears to have cast a blight upon the creation itself! Alas, the creation itself groaneth with the rebellion of God's very own people! Yet, even with this widespread conspicuous damage, we must dig deeper to find the prime mover of such spiritual carnage. The manifestation of a stagnant and stale smell in a room is never the cause itself, but merely the symptom of the source of a more sublime mold or mildew. Most of the time this insidious culprit exists beyond our common eyesight while lying just beneath the surface. In verse 11, we find that hidden perpetrator, it is the hedonism of the **religious hierarchy** that had permeated throughout the whole kingdom.

> "For both prophet and priest are profane; yea, **in my house** have I found their wickedness, saith the LORD." (Jeremiah 23:11)

We have an old saying in religious circles that I have heard many times and it goes something like this: "As the pulpit goes, so goes the pew." However, I would even take this a step further and top it off with this statement, "As the pew goes, so goes the world." In these passages in Jeremiah, it's very clear that the damage runs deeper than a few presumptuous pastors unwilling to sell out to God's agenda. No, this proceeds out into the whole of creation and its ripple effects are felt for generations to come.

In modern Christanity, I have observed a great tragedy unfold. I would liken it to a search party in search of a missing child. As they scour the nearby landscape for hours calling the child's name until they reach the point of exhaustion, the fear of a tragedy grows. They come to find out, by a later discovery, that the child was asleep in the house the whole time in a place where they normally would not lay down. Since it was not their normal routine to sleep in that spot, the searchers failed to actually look in that location.

Like that perceivably lost child, so has it been with the modern church. They comb the political landscape of (their own party) for some semblance of righteousness whereby they may place their stock in, while all the while shouting spiritual profanities at (the other party) with the lesser "good moral qualities." They look everywhere in the **outside world** for the blame of their own spiritual declension, except for the one true place it is hiding, right within the pulpit in front of them. Notice in that 11th verse where the searching eyes of "He who is invisible" found the hindrance! "**IN MY HOUSE** have I found their wickedness, saith the LORD."

The Lord always traces everything back to His high office. He knows where the true blame lies. It lies at the door of the house of God. Judgment must begin here. Beloved, we are forced to ask ourselves a question: "Is the righteous judge of all the earth able to judge the world without an appropriate standard?" The answer may not be so cut and dry. Yes, He is God and He is absolute in His Judgements upon humanity. And, of course it needs go unsaid that God will ultimately judge all of humanity at the end of all things, according to the amount of light they have received.

Nevertheless, His ***standard i***n the earth currently, is His ***representative*** body. When the light is cast in its full luminescence on the earth, emanating from his holy bride, the darkness becomes more apparent.

This righteous God loves for ***His righteousness*** to reside within the sacred bench of the clergy. "Do you not know ye shall judge angels?" (see 1 Corinthians 6:3). When the pulpit fails to hold high the standard of God's righteous law as the convincing element of His holy nature, it fails to allow room for conviction of humanities crimes against Him. And where there is no conviction, there are no true conversions. If we lean on our governmental institutions to legislate morality and attempt to create our Christian utopia from the steps of a Capitol Hill, or a parliamentary palace, we grossly fail. Those entities were never intended for such use and cannot hold the standard high when the church has lessened theirs. God has not sent His Son into the world to save governmental systems, countries, or kingdoms. He was rather sent to save individuals by transforming them from the inside out. All other attempts to "moralize" man is an exercise in futility. No more can this approach change a human being, than it could change an aggressive pit bull by placing it in a restrictive compound, in hopes to give it the nature of the more docile labrador retriever.

The gospel must be preached in convincing power upon the stubborn heart of rebellious mankind for him to have any opportunity of a true change. This alone can bring that proper conviction necessary to break that towering citadel of mankind's pride down to his knees. The anarchy burning within our own bosom calls for such a desperate probing and this alone will cause it to turn loose of its own rulership. We monsters of iniquity must be convinced of our high treason before a just and holy God before we can truly see our need for redemption.

In the modern church, the ***cross of Jesus Christ*** is being held out prematurely. Much like a summer flu shot, the masses are presented with the remedy far before the onslaught of the virus of sin is even detected. The pulpit must return to true righteousness preaching under the unction of the Spirit. This alone will take us beyond the topical conversions of today and return us to the necessary travail and true manifestations of biblical repentance of yesteryear.

Let us allow the apostle Paul to carry us out of this chapter with his lovely commendation to the lamenting Corinthian church. In light of his first letter and its scathing rebuke, he undergirds them in their gracious response in his second one that he would send to them.

> "For behold this self same thing, that ye sorrowed after a godly sort, what carefulness it wrought in you, yea, what *clearing* of yourselves, yea, what *indignation*, yea, what *fear*, yea, what vehement desire, yea, what *zeal*, yea, what *revenge*! In all things ye have approved yourselves to be clear in this matter." (2 Corinthians 7:11)

May the pulpits also deal with the number one matter at hand thusly, and receive this same wonderful result that Paul did! Broken hearts before God, ready to move on into His fullness!

## Chapter 10

# GRACE: A LICENSE?

*"And come and stand before me in this house,
which is called by my name, and say, We are delivered
to do all these abominations? Jeremiah 7:10*

THERE IS A WORD in the book of God that seems to afford much ambiguity these days as to its exact meaning. Many doctrines, both true and false, have been built upon this little stone of a word that lies in the midst of the foundation of this great gospel building called the church. This word in the Greek vernacular is called **charis**, but we know it to be interpreted in our vernacular as **grace**. No word in the Bible has been more misused, misinterpreted, and treated in a more abusive manner than has this word grace. It has come to be known as being defined in modern terms as "unmerited favor." However, I feel that at this point in time, especially in light of these said abuses, we need to revisit its meaning. An entire book could be written right here at this juncture, yet it would not be adequately sufficient to remove all the modern misgivings of this beautiful word. Nonetheless, we will at least devote a couple chapters in our attempt to recapture its true definition.

Returning to Jeremiah chapter 23, we find in verse 14 that the Lord is proclaiming His feelings most expressly concerning what He sees in the prophets of Jerusalem.

"I have seen also in the prophets of Jerusalem an horrible thing: they commit adultery, and walk in lies: they strengthen also the hands of evildoers, that none doth return from his wickedness: they are all of them unto me as Sodom, and the inhabitants thereof as Gomorrah." (Jeremiah 23:14)

Allow us to focus on this part of the verse that implies the misuse of that sacred office of a prophet. In light of this text, we must ask ourselves the following questions: What must have been the specific message that was being propagated to the people? What was being conveyed which would result in God handing down such indictments as these two following accusations? "They **strengthen the hands of the evil doers**, that **none doth return** from his wickedness."

These results have to imply none other than a false covering of some kind, coupled with a message that would soothe the unbridled conscience of evildoers. It wasn't only the sin committed by the prophets and priests themselves that drew the ire of the Most High, but the **EFFECT** of such sin upon the laity as well. How do the hands of evildoers become strengthened? It can only be by removing the seriousness of their crime from their consciences.

These prophets, as a result of the sin within their own hearts, had laid aside the searching message of conviction and gave way to the tolerance for sin. Herein lies one of the biggest tragedies in the house of God….when iniquity is excused and allowed to thrive. When the message preached has within it a built in scapegoat for sin, such as the modern false grace message does, it can afford nothing else than a tolerance for wrongdoing. This high crime of the defrocking of the word grace from its original purpose and meaning has damaged more souls than any other attempt of the devil to tear down the body of Christ.

## GRACE: A LICENSE?

If we leap ahead to the 16th and the 17th verse, here, we will see something quite telling as to the motivation of these prophets and the end result of such teaching:

> "Thus saith the LORD of hosts, Hearken not unto the words of the prophets that prophesy unto you: they ***make you vain***: they speak a vision of ***their own heart,*** *and* not out of the mouth of the LORD. They say still unto them that ***despise me***, The LORD hath said, ***Ye shall have peace***; and they say unto every one that walketh after the imagination of his own heart, ***no evil shall come upon you.***" (Jeremiah 23:16-17)

Two things become clear in these passages. Firstly, the words spoken by these pillow prophets have produced a vanity within the hearers. This vanity is no other than an empty message which can only produce an empty experience. When the fear of God is stripped from the pulpit, it translates to the pew. These men were no doubt preaching a "relatable God" that focused more upon the beneficial blessings and one who turned His head at iniquity. This empty form of preaching pervades within the modern church to unprecedented proportions. It is a gospel that comes from the heart of man and produces no holy fruit within the recipient.

Secondly, and probably the most alarming aspect of this false grace, is the promise of peace in the 17th verse. This false peace was promised to a people who did not meet the criteria of true repentance from sin.

Now, you may pause right here and ask, how does this pertain to me if the prophet is here speaking of "them who despise me?" You may object by saying something like this: "I do not despise God. I go to church and pray and carry on a normal religious life. I also consider myself a person with high morals." Allow me to elaborate on this point so as to establish the nature of this indictment handed down by the Most High.

There are many ways to despise God other than a blatant outward display of brazen, adulterous activity, or for that matter, any other visible manifestation of sin. Notice who is being spoken to here: "Every one that walketh after the *imagination* of his own heart." The Spirit of the Lord always goes beyond the topical and cuts deep between the joints and marrow with His quickening word.

Walking with God is a deep, inward display of affection and devotion that cannot always be readily seen in mere outward abstinence. No, a relationship with God is in the inner chambers, deep within the bosom of the human experience. If one walks in the "imagination of their own heart," they are walking in a form of presumption concerning the nature of God. Their relationship is but topical and the bottom line of the devils nature (the spirit of disobedience), has not been slain within them. Peace was here promised by the false prophets to such individuals who were only serving a God of mere observance. A *version* of God who did not move them from their sin, but soothed them, while it yet gripped them in its destructive arms.

Many people may also find themselves making these objections at this point: "We are referring to an Old Testament God here, aren't we? Did He not become a softer, gentler, understanding God in Christ? Surely grace has taken on a more amicable definition in the light of the New Covenant?" Let us advance centuries to a New Testament prophet who spoke of this same tragedy of false grace within the boundaries of the New Covenant. This same New Covenant, by the way, which makes greater demands on humanity due to the accommodation within the power of the risen Christ!

In that short, yet prophetically poignant book of Jude over in the New Testament, we can read of this destructive force of false grace bullying its way into the sacred halls of God's house. If dynamite comes in

## GRACE: A LICENSE?

small packages, surely Jude's scathing warnings attest to this truth. He warns emphatically of a coming storm. Not a storm of natural sciences, but a spiritual storm of demonic forces pushing against the sacred doors of the church. In verses 3 and 4 of this single chapter book filled with futuristic fury, he pulls no punches in this boxing match with the angels of light. Allow us to observe his ringside instructions:

> "Beloved, when I gave all diligence to write unto you of the common salvation, it was needful for me to write unto you, and exhort *you* that ye should **earnestly contend** for the faith which was once delivered unto the saints. For there are certain men crept in unawares, who were before of old ordained to this condemnation, ungodly men, turning the **grace of our God into lasciviousness**, and denying the only Lord God, and our Lord Jesus Christ." (Jude 1:3-4)

Here, our sacred writer informs us of a fight that is constantly taking place for the very soul of the Christian faith. This assault of godless men would ever exist as a threat to the church and Jude would warn of the ever present risk of them creeping insidiously under the very doors of the church. The encroachment of these entities would be as an unseen vine that moves slowly and methodical enough so as to remain undetected. This "contending for the faith" that Jude prods the church over was quite clearly an attempt to hold fast the "doctrine according to godliness" (see 1 Timothy 6:3). The grace of God would be the victim, and the assailant would be Satan's very own agents sent to wrest this wonderful word.

The goal of these hordes of hell is a very pinpointed effort to bring distortion to the sacred truth of the transforming power of God's grace. Consequently, through this systematic breakdown, grace would be turned into a *license* of sorts. In turning the grace of God into lasciviousness, this goal would be achieved. This word **lasciviousness** has a wide range of usage and makes an inference to immorality and a looseness towards all things holy. We could best sum it up by describing it as a "**license to sin.**"

The warning here is emphatic and clarion as to the protocol for the church to counter such an assault on truth. We must *fight* for it! Contend for this faith once delivered! We can no longer let this sacred definition be redefined by smooth talking devils! Sin is still sin, and sin is still the problem. Better yet, grace is still the answer to overcome that dastardly Devil who ardently seeks an abiding presence in the bosom of the church. "Where sin abounds, grace doth much more abound!" (see Romans 5:20).

If we would make an overall assessment of the majority of the modern pulpits concerning their approach to grace, we would find an uncanny similarity to a set of Old Testament verses. Not only can we see the admonition of Jude being relevant to our time, but, we can also see that this problem goes all the way back to the rebellious children of Israel as well. As we again turn to our weeping prophet, we find this insidious mode of thinking permeating throughout God's people to the point of ultimate delusion.

> "Behold, ye trust in lying words, that cannot profit. Will ye steal, murder, and commit adultery, and swear falsely, and burn incense unto Baal, and walk after other gods whom ye know not; And come and stand before me in this house, which is called by my name, and say, **We are delivered to do all these abominations?** Is this house, which is called by my name, become a den of robbers in your eyes? Behold, even I have seen *it*, saith the LORD." (Jeremiah 7:8-11)

Notice the offset of this particular set of verses? "Lying words, that cannot profit." Herein lies the most troublesome reality of this admonition from the Lord. It is the fact that this type of message cannot advance man towards God, but rather, alienates him from his Creator. The recipients of this rebuke were continuing in all things unlawful and offensive to a holy God, yet, were trusting in the covering of sacrificial offerings to create a false buffer zone between the Lord and His people. It is evident that these people had ***not given up*** their sin at all, yet, expected God to ***overlook*** them due to the fact that they had been ***forgiven.*** Instead of the gratitude and change of heart that should spring from a heart forgiven and washed of their old infractions, they used His mercy as a catapult into further iniquity.

Isaiah would echo this same sentiment in the 59th chapter of his book when he would write the words of the Spirit to a rebellious nation. The Lord would incriminate the Jewish nation over their complaints regarding His turned face from their pompous pleadings. He would show them that the true problem lie with them, and not with the Righteous Judge of all the earth.

> "Behold, the LORD'S hand is not shortened, that it cannot save; neither his ear heavy, that it cannot hear: But your iniquities have separated between you and your God, and ***your sins*** have ***hid His face*** from you, that He ***will not hear.***" (Isaiah 59:1-2)

In this passage, we see a Creator extended, and a creature disconnected. The Lord's ability to save can never be in question, due the length of His divine reach, and the openness of His heavenly hearing. No, the deficit truly lies on our end, always. With man's murky view obscuring his inner eyesight, he becomes oblivious to this yearning and reconciliatory plea coming down from his Creator. Oh! How easily God could remove the barriers between us! How quickly would "the blood of Jesus Christ His Son cleanse us from all sin!" (see 1 John 1:7). Oh, if we would but embrace it, if we would but believe it, if we would but receive it!

This false notion, of a false grace, bringing man into a false position, has reigned supreme within the pacifying pulpits of compromise for eons, it seems. It is high time for the church to turn over every rock where this slippery serpent of compromise may be hiding. Let us hunt out incessantly all defilements of its effects on the church and cut the head off of its faith numbing ability to bite our heels. May we bruise it most ruthlessly, without the sympathy of its writhing under the force of our feet.

May we turn away from this modern monster of false grace that has been manufactured in the lab of Lucifer himself. These entities have been flown unabashedly as doctrinal dirty birds into the church's bell towers to nest. The offspring which has hatched out of these nests, is a grace that affords us false peace and proclaims, "God does not see us in the performance of our sins, for we are covered by His grace and hidden from His eyes under the blood of His Son." Oh, let us cast aside such abominable definitions and recapture the glorious essence of this wondrous word called grace! Follow me to the next chapter for its true definition.

Chapter 11

# GRACE: A LIBERATION

*"What shall we say then? Shall we continue in sin,
that grace may abound? God forbid. How shall we,
that are dead to sin, live any longer therein?" Romans 6:1-2*

SOME 35 YEARS PRIOR TO WRITING THIS BOOK, a glorious truth began to unfold to me within the sacred text of God's word. This truth was the fact that within the gospel promises, there awaits a victorious life to be had by all. As I poured over this new found revelation I discovered that the book of God, was in essence, one big promise. This promise consisted of an opportunity for man to walk with God in a glorious union with Himself. It would be so intimate of a union, that through this indwelling Christ, we could walk above the powers of sin. Not, of course, in a state of **perfection** that would render us **incapable of a fall**, but the sustaining essence of God that would make true that wonderful text in 1st Peter 1:5, "Who are kept by the power of God."

It was at this crossroad of my life as a new believer that God began to uncover the true meaning of grace to my heart. I believe He chose to share this great truth with this hungry fledgling at that time, due to my complete openness to His truth. I poured over the verses, only to find that this word grace, took on a far more in-depth meaning than just the typical "unmerited favor" description I had previously heard among the Christian circles.

Around that same time, my father-in-law had placed an original "Strong's Exhaustive Concordance" in my hands, not the "Strongest Strong's" edition that would come after the original, but the one that was untouched by the more modern interpretations of "***higher***" learning. Right after I received it, I immediately took advantage of digging into the meaning of this word called grace.

I was stunned with elation when I found that the definition would confirm what the Lord had already laid upon my heart. As I traced down the original definition, there it was before me in all its glory! "***The divine influence upon the heart, and its reflection in the life.***" I marveled at the sheer reality of what the Lord had been showing this young heart of the true essence of the gospel, and how He was now confirming it. This caused me to beam with excitement and a new hope rushed into my very being.

I then began to see a new theme unfolding in the book of God. That theme was that this grace was an ***effect*** and an influence that was tangible, rather than just a ***favor*** that God arbitrarily bestows upon the masses. When I began to interchange the word grace with the phrase "divine influence," I immediately perceived that this definition was the much better fit, as opposed to the more popular use of "unmerited favor." It now started to seem evident to me that a ***sabotage*** of sorts had taken place in the modern church.

During this time of discovery, I began to notice a missing piece within this grand puzzle called Christendom. It was the ominous reality that whenever grace was mentioned among church folk, the word seemed to always be shortchanged. I took mental notes in certain circles whenever I heard the word coupled with the common phrases of the day. These were phrases such as, "No worries about obedience anymore, we are not under law, but under grace," and the ever popular, "I'm just a sinner saved by grace." There were many other phrases that set off my alarm, but these two examples will suffice in order to make the point. I remember thinking how these types of phrases began to lean more toward an **EXCUSE** for sin, rather than a **POWER** to overcome it. I saw that indeed grace had been turned into a false covering for an ***uncrucified lifestyle*** as opposed to an ***influence unto righteousness*** that the book of God made claim of.

Let it be said by the writer right here, that within the meaning of grace, there is indeed a *favor* bestowed upon the individual who receives it. As it could also be said that one cannot *earn* it with any attempts at personal righteousness. However, if we stop short with this definition of "unmerited favor" alone, we might as well be using a lightning bolt for an umbrella. If we try to pervert the provisional power of God and thereby turn it into a compromised covering, we have but reduced it to mere sand that passes through our fingers. It is quite clear that within the pages of the word of God, there is a meaning of grace that needs to be revisited, one that is chomping at the bit to come forth again into the light! If we look at a couple of passages in the powerful book of Titus, we can easily see this hidden gem shining amongst the rubble of our watered down modern vernacular. Let's indulge, shall we?

> "For the grace of God that bringeth salvation hath appeared to all men, Teaching us that, denying ungodliness and worldly lusts, we should live soberly, righteously, and godly, in this present world." (Titus 2:11-12)

Voila! Here is the great unveiling of true grace! Based upon these passages, we find it is indeed an influence, a power, a persuasion, and an innate compulsion by the Spirit to perform that which is right! This *appearance* is none other than the risen Christ Himself! The very nature of God Himself, translated into the bosom of man, lived out by divine force, and engulfed in the flames of true love. This denying of all things ungodly is not a mere outward formality, nay, it is the dynamic result of a co-union with a living Christ.

The word *"teaching"* is not used here as we use the word in regard to academics. It is not here referring to acquiring knowledge from a source of information, but rather, it is an inference to an inward persuasion, wrought in the heart by the Holy Ghost. The following verse from the apostle John will help us drive this point home:

> "But the anointing which ye have received of Him abideth in you, and ye need not that any man teach you: but as the same anointing *teacheth* you of all things, and is truth, and is no lie, and even as it hath taught you, ye shall abide in him." (1 John 2:27)

This word "teaching" mentioned in these two separate epistles alludes to something that transcends the mental faculties and finds it lodging within our spirit. The desired effect of this teaching is that of a deposit being made. Clearly, the apostle is here referring to a *conveyance* and *transfer* of sorts, as opposed to the experience of *acquiring knowledge*. How else could we have this result of "denying ungodliness and living soberly, righteously, and godly" in this present dreadful condition in which we live, except there be a power manifested in this experience? This anointing can be none other than a grace that moves, a grace that purifies, and a grace that sanctifies.

Some may here raise the following objection, "Well, aren't we saved by grace and not by anything we do? Doesn't there have to then be an official declaration based on us just believing?" To that I would say, indeed, grace comes, not by merit, just as the scripture states. However, are we then supposing that grace is a ***divine positional declaration*** and an unmerited favor that the Lord simply ascribes to our account upon believing? To clear up the murky waters that are running through the landscape of the modern church on this subject, let's take a closer look at this famously mishandled verse in Ephesians to see if we can address such a question:

> "For by grace are ye saved through faith; and that not of yourselves: *it is* the gift of God: Not of works, lest any man should boast. For we are **His workmanship**, created in Christ Jesus unto good works, which God hath before ordained that we should walk in them." (Ephesians 2:8-10)

So then, if this grace affords a salvation, which by definition is a real change by the "***workmanship***" of God Himself, then surely a dynamic transfer must take place. By this language, is it not evident that if something is being "***created*** in Christ Jesus unto good works" that a manifest power of righteousness must break forth? If something is being ***saved,*** can we not assume that there must be practical ***rescue*** involved?

Imagine a great ship that has been broken apart from the furious waves of an angry sea. The passengers, now in peril for their very life, would desperately seek out any form of flotation device they could locate. Would they not grope for everything from lifeboats, parts of the ship, even to each other? They would make no assessment as to the nature of the item in which they cling to, nor the exact longevity of its ability to sustain them at sea. No! Their only concern would be to survive the moment and so find themselves escaping the immediacy of the imminent danger.

This is where true grace enters. These desperate people can afford nothing of mere **positional safety**. Neither can they trust in a fanciful declaration from the captain who calls out the phrase, "All is well, dear passengers, if you will but just believe the ship is not truly sinking, you will be saved!" Never could they lean upon such treason of their trust! Never! These poor souls are convinced of the unfolding reality that they are sinking into the murky depths and they need something beyond a false assurance, they need a **RESCUE**! Their only hope is that someone pulls them from their certain death with a rescuing arm of salvation. To tell them they are saved by mere **proclamation and declaration** would be as deceptive as to toss them blankets and tell them to "cover up with these, for they will save your lives."

Such it is with the gospel. The grace of God is the very **influence** that moves into the drowning heart of a dying man and supplies him with that divine lifeboat for his rescue. It is the voice of power and authority that speaks to the turbulent storm of man's spirit at conversion! Oh, how this grace goes far beyond favor, or a covering for iniquities! It is the very essence of Christ Himself, communicated to the desperate heart that has come face to face with its own sinking condition. There, His marvelous influence converts the sinner by the power of His revealed sacrifice. Then, in reflection of the inward transformation, that life is then transferred in the shiny countenance of one forgiven and emancipated. Consequently, the outward life automatically manifests His zealous works! Let us consider another couple of passages from our dear apostle Paul in the powerful book of Romans:

> "Moreover, the law entered, that the offense might abound. But where sin abounded, grace **did much more abound**: That as sin hath reigned unto death, even so might **grace reign**

***through righteousness*** unto eternal life by Jesus Christ our Lord." (Romans 5:20-21)

In these passages in Romans, there is a very emphatic reference to the trumping power of grace over sin. In other words, as iniquity built its citadel of obstinate power within the human condition over the course of time, grace was waiting in the wings to manifest in the person of Christ. This abundance of grace displaces the abundance of sin! This provision must certainly be a power that trumps the lesser of the two. As powerful as sin has become in the human experience, it's no match for the flowing power of the nature of Jesus Christ that cascades down into the truly repentant heart. Here in the verse above, Paul states that "grace reigns through righteousness." Whatever could this mean if grace is merely a covering or simply a favor bestowed upon humanity? It is clear that this grace is a ***righteous influence*** that has nothing less than a tangible manifested display in the heart and soul.

Oh beloved, may we see that the power of God in the person of Christ is able to overcome all sin and rebellion in the human heart. The provision is indeed there, awaiting our appropriation by pure, unadulterated faith. Grace **IS** Jesus, and Jesus **IS** grace! He **IS** the influence of the divine that we must experience within our hearts! Let us receive Him in His full capacity to overcome that serpent in our bosom!

I would like to conclude this chapter with an appeal. That appeal is for us to reconsider our definitions of grace and how we have perceived it in a very weak light. Let us revisit the idea that God's grace, through the indwelling Christ, is nothing less than a provision that supersedes the prevailing power of sin within our hearts. He is the provision that enables us to overcome its insidious reign, through the power and influence of divine love within the heart. Let us close with this wonderful declaration from our dear apostle Paul as he shows us the enabling power of God's grace.

> "But by the grace of God I am what I am: and His grace which was bestowed upon me was not in vain; but I labored more abundantly than they all: yet not I, but the grace of God which was with me." (1 Corinthians 15:10)

# Chapter 12

# FAITH: FACT OR FICTION?

*"The just shall live by faith."* Romans 1:17

IN THE MODERN ERA OF CHRISTIANITY, possibly no word has been spoken of more than the word ***faith***. If there has been one book written on it, there have seemingly been a million. This five letter word has likely been interjected in practically every sermon ever preached at one point or another. So with that said, consider this: If you were an enemy of God would you not go after the definition of such a word? If you were Satan, would you not make a very consorted and pinpointed effort to pervert one of Christianity's most sacred words? Certainly you would.

If you go on a simple search online, you will find a couple of definitions of faith. These explanations of faith are neatly packaged for our consideration. They are as follows:

1. Complete trust or confidence in someone or something.

2. Strong belief in God or in the doctrines of a religion, based on spiritual apprehension rather than proof.

Now, most would concur with these definitions as sufficient to describe the faith that they may be engaging in at this very moment. When asked this simple entry level question: "Do you believe in God?" most would likely respond in a manner such as: "Of course I believe in God, this all didn't happen out of nothing, therefore, there has to be a Creator." These types of replies would flow from their lips with great ease and certainty. When pressed a little deeper on the issue of personal religion, most will quickly reach for the nearest garment of **confession** to wrap around their exposed and vulnerable frame, as no one wants to be caught naked without a religious cloak, ever!

If I were to ask a general question, such as the following one, for example: "Would you consider yourself to be religious in any way?" This would likely trigger a response such as: "I go to church, of course I'm religious." Or the famous response of: "I was baptized as a child, I am therefore in good standing with God." It may even go so far as a declaration of this sort: "I went down to an altar at a church once and repeated a sinner's prayer after the dictates of a preacher, therefore, I am sealed." Not to mention the classic response of: "Oh yes, **my** faith is very strong, I couldn't have made it this far, if I didn't have strong beliefs!" When entreated in such a manner, these textbook answers are almost always a slam dunk guarantee as to what may come out of the mouths of the confessors and professors of religion in this modern church age. These answers would all quickly and unquestionably be deemed as "faith" in one form or another.

Now, in light of all those above mentioned points, let us take this opportunity to go beyond these **nominal** definitions of faith and dig a little deeper. As we consider biblical New Testament faith from the view of scripture, perhaps we can glean a more practical understanding of this much used word. It's an unquestionable reality that Jesus would be the highest expert on the nature of faith, as He is the very "author and finisher" (see Hebrews 12:2) of such. When we delve into the gospel account of the Lord's dealings with His disciples concerning the nature of faith, it becomes evident that those boys knew little, if anything, of the essence of divine faith. His educational course on faith was nothing within the ballpark of most modern teachings on faith. In fact, it was just the opposite.

In Matthew chapter 14, we have one of those particular accounts in which Jesus is able to show the distinction between **human** faith and ***divine*** faith. We must remember that many of these events were actually "divine setups" and thereby an opportunity for Jesus to expose the frailty of man and his need for divine influence in all things, including faith itself. Allow us to look at the account:

> And Peter answered Him and said, Lord, if it be thou, bid me come unto thee on the water. And He said, Come. And when Peter was come down out of the ship, he walked on the water, to go to Jesus. But when he saw the wind boisterous, he was afraid; and beginning to sink, he cried, saying, Lord, save me. And immediately Jesus stretched forth *His* hand, and caught him, and said unto him, O thou of little faith, wherefore didst thou doubt? And when they were come into the ship, the wind ceased. Then they that were in the ship came and worshipped Him, saying, Of a truth thou art the Son of God." (Mathew 14:28-33)

Dare I say, of the myriads of sermons that have been preached on this particular account, there have likely been precious few that have captured the true gist of it. I can speak for the ones that I have heard on the subject, at least. Most would point out here that Peter is making the fatal mistake of taking his eyes off of Jesus and looking at the conditions surrounding him. Consequently, he would find himself sinking into the ominous waves.

However, I feel that we need to dig a little deeper here into the **rebuke** uttered by the master for a more telling disclosure of the main point. We notice here, Jesus did not say: "Peter, why did you take your eyes off of me and look at the tumultuous waves surrounding you? Why did you not keep your eyes steadfastly upon me?" No, it wasn't the **FOCUS** at all that was the problem, it was rather placing trust in the **WRONG** thing that sank this zealous disciple! "O thou of **LITTLE** faith, wherefore didst thou doubt?"

The Lord would often ask questions that He already knew the answer to, and this was no exception. This question, "Why did you doubt?" proceeded from the master's lips in order to show Peter the root cause of this failure of footwork upon the waters surface. He was all too aware of Peter's **self-dependency.** Over the course of their 3½ year tenure together, He would rebuke him betimes for his reliance on his own innate constitutional fortitude. So, what was Jesus getting at here? Was it a lack of faith? Was it a misdirected eyesight? I would submit for your consideration that it was neither. I believe it can be clearly shown that it was rather a *wrong kind* of faith that He was here addressing.

Many times in the gospel accounts we have the Lord chastising the disciples (as well as humanity in general for that matter), for their "*little faith*." We have been erroneously taught in the modern era that this phrase is referring to the fact that we must have *our* faith increased. However, it is not the *size* of faith that was being addressed here at all, but it was the fact that Peter was trying to use his **HUMAN** faith to achieve a **DIVINE** goal. The first few steps of this tempestuous walk on the water went off without a hitch. But, it wasn't because it came from anything **within** Peter himself, oh no, but rather to the contrary. The faith that afforded him such a brevity of bravery came through the divine stream of his hearing of but one word: "***COME!***"

"Faith cometh **BY** hearing." (Romans 10:17)

When the Son of God spoke that one word, the very essence of faith was within its syllables! This is what gave this future apostle the solid footing that was needed to walk on water as if it were thick glass, it was *A WORD*! Peter's response was spontaneous because of the bidding of His master. That water-walking-faith did not come from **Peter himself** at all. It came rather from ***Jesus Himself!*** That "little" faith that caused Peter to ultimately sink and invoke the rescuing arm of the Savior, wasn't adequate for buoyancy. He needed a supernatural faith to afford that walk of fame upon the tumultuous sea. He needed the faith ***OF*** Jesus, not merely faith ***IN*** Jesus to be able to make such a journey.

You may say at this point, "What does it matter about faith and its origin and such? Aren't we called by God to just believe, and all things will be possible? I mean, what does it matter if it's faith *in* Jesus or the faith *of* Jesus?" To that objection I would pose these questions: Did it matter to Jesus? Was it important that He conveyed this origin of faith to His disciples? Did His rebuking of *small* faith have any value at all in His mentioning of it?

Allow us to look into another account in the gospels to get our answers. Here, in Luke 17, we have a request from the apostles that would seem on the surface as having the appearance of being quite noble in its nature. Let us observe:

> The apostles said unto the Lord, "***Increase our faith***." And the Lord said, "***If ye had faith*** as a grain of mustard seed, ye

might say unto this sycamine tree, be thou plucked up by the root, and be thou planted in the sea; and it should obey you." (Luke 17:5-6)

Several years ago, I found myself in fellowship with a small assembly of believers that were very serious seekers of the Lord and His truth. This gracious man of God at the helm would share his pulpit with me and allow me to share what I felt at the time to be the truths that the Lord was disclosing to me. During my tenure there, something incredible dawned on me. This beloved pastor friend of mine would often preach on this passage out of Luke 17. I can recall the struggle I had with the comprehension of just exactly what he was trying to bring across the pulpit concerning this passage. After the clouds finally lifted and I saw clearly the revelation of it, consequently, it turned out to be one of the most incredible spiritual lightbulb moments I have ever experienced.

It astonished me that out of all the times I had read those passages, I had never seen the true essence of it. As my pastor friend would stand and say incessantly, "If **YOU** had faith the size of…." He would always emphasize the **YOU** part of the verse and I would struggle in my mind to grasp the concept, although I just couldn't get it. I now realize in hindsight of those moments that my judgment was clouded by the religious devils of my past. Unbeknownst to me, those foul birds of doctrinal diversion had programmed me to believe in the perverted view of faith. A faith that had to be ***mustered*** up, a faith that had to be pushed out beyond my own carnal limitations, a faith that needed to be "***increased***."

Finally, during one of those particular sermons, the light suddenly came on! Jesus wasn't talking about ***the size*** of our faith at all, rather, He was talking about ***the kind*** of faith! "Little faith" was so long referred to from modern pulpits as a faith that needed to be ***exercised and utilized*** in order to grow. As a result, I had never been able to see the forest for all the trees in the way. It finally dawned on me that Jesus was actually here denouncing human engineered faith and its being inadequate to produce anything of supernatural origin. When the disciples asked Him to "increase" their faith, His response was basically along these lines, and I paraphrase:

> "Boys, I cant increase **YOUR** faith, it's not possible to do so. Your faith is not made of the right stuff. But, if you had **MY FAITH** it wouldn't matter the size of it, because my supernatural faith is a consistent substance! It is not measured by volume at all, but rather in substance! And if you had it, you could say to this tree, be uprooted and planted in the sea and it would have to listen to you. It wouldn't even matter if it was the size of a little seed, it would still produce mountainous results."

Let us come face to face with these paramount questions concerning the essence of our very own faith that we are in possession of: Is it indeed divine faith, dealt to you by heavenly hands? Or is it a faith concocted, mustered, and one that stems out of your own toilsome mental faculties? Examine yourself and consider, do you really know this divine faith? Or are you simply walking in a carnal presumptive state that is developed in the factory of your own mind? Has the measure of faith been dealt to you? Have you played the divine card on the table? Or have you been using a fleshly alternative that has in it no real divine connection?

Dear friend, please consider the gravity of this. This is of the utmost importance as to whether you are in possession of the faith **OF** Christ, or simply trying to place faith **IN** Christ. One is an "operation of God" (see Colossians 2:12). The other is a presumptive attempt to reach out of one's own resources in order to touch the fingers of the divine.

> "And because ye are sons, God hath *sent forth* the Spirit of His Son into your hearts, crying, Abba, Father." (Galatians 4:6)

It's by **HIS** faith we can cry "Abba, Father!" It's by His faith we can believe. It's by His faith we can be transformed. It's by His faith, we can walk on water!

And it's by His faith we stand!

## Chapter 13

# FAITH: EVIDENCE OR EMPTINESS?

*"Now faith is the substance of things hoped for, the evidence of things not seen." Hebrews 11:1*

AS WE HAD STATED IN THE PREVIOUS CHAPTER, this thing called *faith* has taken a tremendous barrage of enemy fire over the last few decades. Since the dawn of the *"**word of faith**"* movement, which came on strong in the early eighties, this five letter word has morphed into a magic wand of sorts. These pioneers of presumption erroneously taught that a mere magical mantra and confession of faith was all that was needed to be waved over circumstances in order to bring about one's desired effects. This particular surge of pseudo faith became the catalyst for the dismal doctrines of feigned faith that is pervasive in the church today.

The abuse and perversion of this particular verse in Hebrews 11 in our chapter heading was probably by far the worst of the carnage from this movement. Through this systematic subversion of truth, the "name it and claim it" slogans began to emerge and capture the imagination of the church. It was, by and large, a church that was searching for a legitimate higher place in God's kingdom. However, it quickly became subverted by the mystical idea that "things" could literally be spoken aforetime in faith, and then materialize in the natural world. Although some would see through this peculiar charismatic branding of faith, the damage was all but done. This insidious doctrinal leaven had permeated, in one form or another, through the entirety of the whole loaf.

But enough about that! Let us look at the true thought that the writer of Hebrews here wishes to convey. Again, I think that right here, the Greek definition must enter the equation in order to take us to where we need to go. If we observe this word "***substance***" in this passage closely, we will see a concept emerge that is otherworldly in its implications. It means:

> "properly (to possess) *standing under* a guaranteed agreement ("title-deed")" (source Bible Hub/ Strongs #5287)

Now, at first glance this would appear to be a very simple definition and one that could be taken as a supporter of a "name it and claim it" ideology of faith. The common misunderstanding here is that the "guaranteed agreement" is with the actual **THING** desired rather than with **CHRIST** Himself. Allow us to break it down and see if there is not something a little deeper here. The words that stand out to me here are "to possess." These two words very straightforwardly imply that a transaction has occurred, a passing of one to another, if you will. In the first verse of the second epistle of Peter, the apostle spoke of this very ***possession*** along these lines:

> "Simon Peter, a servant and an apostle of Jesus Christ, to them that have ***obtained like precious faith*** with us through the righteousness of God and our Savior Jesus Christ." (2 Peter 1:2)

## FAITH: EVIDENCE OR EMPTINESS?

There is a little hidden gem of a phrase in this passage that really discloses the whole gist of it. This three word description, "like precious faith," tells of the true origin of this divine faith and is the secret of the mystery of the entire New Testament! The apostle is here speaking about a faith that is communicated in such close proximity that a divine description is needed in order to do it justice! He describes this kind of faith as "precious," which, when extended to the Greek definition, carries the weighty description of the following:

> *"Equally privileged, held in equal honor."* (source: Bible Hub/Strongs #2472)

This description is indicative of a sharing of sorts, a co-ownership of something, and a privilege equally shared with someone else. Notice also the fact that Peter had "obtained" this faith, thereby implying a communication from another source.

You may say at this point, "I don't see why it is important to go over such details about faith, why can't we simply believe in God's word and all will be well?" To that I would simply reply that herein lies the trouble! We have been modernistically mesmerized to believe that faith is simply believing in an unseen substance and thereby being assured that the evidence will manifest! We must return to the biblical understanding that faith is actually **WITHIN** God Himself and that the person of Christ must be present in order for true divine faith to manifest. That unseen "substance" is **GOD HIMSELF** in the person of Christ breaking forth into the heart with divine faith, and hence providing the evidence of His presence by that pure trust rising up in the soul! This is what the Bible calls the "full assurance of faith" (see Hebrews 10:22), and an "unfeigned faith" (see 1 Timothy 1:5). This has been largely misunderstood in the modern church and been replaced by a form of ***humanistic presumption.***

One may ask, "How then do we get such faith, since we are but limited humans gazing through a dark glass trying to see into the divine realm?" To this inquiry I would respond with another question: How did Peter get it? In order to get our answer, let us consider Peter's pilgrimage prior to the resurrection and ascension of Jesus.

This hard-core fisherman with leather hands would be called right off the boat of his very own fishing business at the invitation of the Son of the Most High. With great zeal he immediately dropped his net, forsook all else, and headed into an adventure of a lifetime. That adventure was to literally walk with "God in the flesh" through this decadent, degraded, and despondent state of humanity. As he traveled with his beloved master over the course of those magnificent three and a half years, he likely heard the word "faith" repeated hundreds, if not thousands of times. "Be it according to your faith." "Thy faith hath made thee whole." "If you had faith the size of a mustard seed." These were phrases that would resonate time after time in the ears of Peter as they traveled through those dusty corridors of broken humanity.

What Peter did not know at the time (nor would any of us have known), was that this faith that Jesus operated in was of an origin beyond human capacity. We see it in this disgruntled disciple's many attempts to perform beyond his own means. For example, walking on the water, claiming to be the one single invincible follower when everyone else failed, and, even to the point of being the zealous sword-wielding defender of Jesus Himself. The Spirit of meekness that the Lord was clothed with as He walked all the way to the cross, was a supply unknown to us carnal creatures of self-preservation. This "gold tried in the fire" was the faith of the divine kind, the pure nature of heaven, and the fragrance of true trust. No, it cannot be pulled from the pockets of human experience, nor can it be drawn from the carved-out cisterns of human ingenuity. This faith must be **DEALT** to us by an encounter with the Holy Ghost! (see Romans 12:3). It's a revealing of the divine nature in the person of Jesus Himself! No other way can the soul cry "Abba, Father" (see Romans 8:15) except this faith be an **EXPERIENCE** that goes beyond a mental ascent and penetrates to the core of the recipient.

Judas and company would inevitably come for the Master to lead Him away captive to endure that brutality called Calvary. Peter in his zealous defense of Jesus would himself step forward and swing the sword of vengeance at those hierarchical hypocrites of injustice. He then proceeded to cut off the ear of the servant of the High Priest only to have the Lord replace it and rebuke him for his "stepping up" in defense of the divine mission in which he still knew nothing about (see John 18:10). No doubt his presumption here was that Jesus would commend his zeal and back him up in his endeavors to preserve all things holy. It was likely that this is the point where he truly began to see the otherworldliness of this divine being, one with a nature far outside his own intellectual reach.

A transfer of the supernatural kind was most assuredly needed in order for such a carnal, self-willed zealot, to be able to withstand the coming mission of "preaching the gospel to all the world." But firstly, Peter's inner drive of self-determination had to be exposed through a series of adversities and even would include a threat to his own self-preserved kingdom (i.e. his own flesh). Jesus would tell the disciples to carry a sword with them. However, this weapon was not to be used for *self-defense,* but rather, as a "prop" for the purpose of *self-exposure.* Jesus knew by the gift of knowledge that this rambunctious rebel would manifest that robust nature of self-preservation. There was no way that this man could be a representative of this celestial kingdom that has within it a nature that is contrary to this self-protective disposition of the devil within our bosoms. There would have to be a reckoning with the nature of his master and a certain death would need to come to that old man within him.

Peter would learn an invaluable lesson the hard way through the indelible experience of that bitter denial at the capturing of His master. He would ultimately come to know that he had not within himself the "divine stuff." Later, while standing by a physical fire, he would be thrown into a grand trial by fire and be tested beyond anything he had ever expected. As he warmed himself by the flames of self-preservation, these ominous words would proceed from the lips of a previously solid soldier of divine defense: "I do not know the man" (see Matthew 26:72).

No doubt, Peter was telling the truth right here. This despondent disciple was faced with the reality that he truly did **not** know this man and His otherworldly disposition! This disciple knew Him "after the flesh," yet his spirit was far from Him. Jesus would later confront him in the presence of his peers on that seashore during that famous fish fry. There, before all, He would call him out in public humility to show him that he possessed but an earthy affection for Him. The Lord would earnestly ask him, "Lovest thou me, **MORE** than these?" (see John 21:15). Jesus wasn't here looking for a *yes*, He was rather looking for an admittance, and an emphatic: "I guess I really don't Lord, I thought I had within me that clinging tenacious love that could carry me all the way through, even more than these, but I see I was dreadfully wrong."

On the day of Pentecost, following that wondrous outpouring of the Spirit, that faith-filled fisherman would stand and preach a most memorable sermon. It would be a divine discourse that would drag three-thousand souls into that gospel ship with the net of his very own mouth. This apostle to the circumcision would have a heavenly zeal and divine boldness that he did not have heretofore this pouring in of the wine of the Spirit. This enabling power from on high would be the difference between a human-driven affection that was incapable of overcoming that fear within, and an otherworldly audacity of divine faith sent forth into the heart by the Spirit. This, and this alone, is how Peter would stand that day in the midst of probable persecution and the imminent threat of death from the same, and still be able to proclaim boldly:

> "Ye men of Judaea, and all *ye* that dwell at Jerusalem, be this known unto you, and hearken to my words: For these are not drunken, as ye suppose, seeing it is *but* the third hour of the day. But **THIS IS THAT** which was spoken by the prophet Joel." (Acts 2:14-16)

Oh, don't you see it friend?! ***This is that*** which was spoken several hundred years beforehand. The Spirit of God would now have His place in the inner courts of man's temple! With Him, would come His most marvelous divine nature in which we could now partake of in a spiritual intimacy! All the virtues of this lofty God, which were but previously observable only from our carnal perspective, would now become an inner reality. This habitation of the Holy One would afford us the experience of **KNOWING** God in an intimate union of the human and the divine. Only then, could we possess that saving faith that is the conduit of all heavenly blessings. "**EVERY GOOD AND PERFECT GIFT** is from **ABOVE,** And cometh **DOWN FROM** the Father of lights!" (see James 1:17).

Let us not leave out our dear apostle to the Gentiles in his quest to convey these very same truths. This hero of the faith knew all too well where the source of virtue proceeded from. In Acts chapter nine, Paul too would experience his very own destiny with self-degradation on the road to Damascus. On this delusional journey of ridding the world of that pesky Christian sect, he would be met with the bright light of this virtuous One in which he was ignorantly opposing. This atomic attitude adjustment would lay bare his own self-righteousness! There upon the dust, from which mankind was formed, he saw "Him who he persecuted" and consequently, saw his own inadequacy. Paul's reaction to the cataclysmic event says it all:

> "And he trembling and astonished said, Lord, what wilt thou have me to do?" (Acts 9:6)

Ananias would be sent by Jesus Himself to pray over this beleaguered zealot to receive his sight back and to receive the Holy Ghost. As the scales fell from his eyes he was baptized and received meat after three days of fasting and prayer. That supernatural faith from heaven filled his heart and transformed a Christian killer into a fiery and fiesty defender of all things righteous. This metamorphosis of such an ominous tyrant of misdirected religious zeal, would turn the Chistian world upside down!

Much later in his ministry, Paul would speak of the death of his self man. That consuming fire of the Holy Ghost would burn up all things within him that he had leaned upon up to that point. If we look close enough within this following verse in Galatians, we can see one of those little words that can change the dynamics of the entire New Testament:

> "I am crucified with Christ: nevertheless I live; yet not I, but Christ liveth in me: and the life which I now live in the flesh I live by the faith **OF** the Son of God, who loved me, and gave Himself for me." (Galatians 2:20)

## FAITH: EVIDENCE OR EMPTINESS?

Do you see it? Hidden there amidst this famous scripture is the pivotal word of the entire New Testament. That little word is "***OF***." Although most modern translations have altered this word to "***IN***," I think the word "***OF***" fits into the theme of New Testament faith much better. Not typically being a fan of other translations other than the KJV, I will make an exception here and call upon the Berean Literal Bible, due to its excellent handling of this verse.

> "I have been crucified with Christ, and I no longer live, but Christ lives in me. And that which I now live in *the* flesh, I live through faith ***from*** the Son of God, the *One* having loved me and having given up Himself for me." (Galatians 2:20)

I simply love the wording that the translators chose here: "Through faith ***from*** the Son of God." This ever important truth, that the divine faith that we have need of is imparted by the very Spirit of God Himself, is what divides the "haves" from the "have-nots." Let us consider always that "He that hath, more shall be given." (see Matthew 13:12). Beloved, let us not settle for presumption. May we fully understand that it is the sustaining power of one, other than ourselves, that we need dwelling within us. And consequently, a faith that is divine, otherworldly, and tried in the fire. None other than the faith ***OF*** the very Son of God! May we not come short of true saving faith, and may we heed this ever important admonition of the apostle Paul:

> "Examine yourselves, whether ye ***be in the faith***; prove your own selves. Know ye not your own selves, how that Jesus Christ is in you, except ye be reprobates?" (2 Corinthians 13:5)

# Chapter 14

# LOVE: TOLERANCE OR TRUTH?

*"If ye love me, keep my commandments." John 14:15*

IN THE MODERN LANDSCAPE OF CHRISTIANITY, there is yet another word that Satan has snatched from the sacred garden of the church. While the overseers had their heads turned, he proceeded to take this word to his own greenhouse of hybrid horticulture and cross pollinate it with his own produce. He then brought in a new mixture of this little word called **LOVE** that he himself cultivated in his soil of seduction. Leaving it on the doorstep of the vulnerable church, she readily gathered it up and proudly displayed it in her sunny window ledges for the world to see.

The modern church now finds itself in the very precarious position of being smack dab in the middle of an age of tolerance, political correctness, and concession. As a result of giving in to these societal pressures, it has been forced, so it would seem, in many ways to forsake the absolutes of truth and sanctity. Here, the church must navigate softly on the eggshells of a politically correct landscape. The famed (501c3) appeal would create a perfect environment for such an insidious canker to grow in her sweet orchard. "Keep all your money, but we want some say among ya" became the swap that the church didn't even see coming.

The thought of being able to have and to hold the entire basket was too big of a temptation for her floundering faith. Through the love of money, this root of evil would fester among her faithful and grow into a plant unimaginable in its scope and size. While the lights were low and the music played softly, this fungus insidiously permeated throughout her fruit supplies. As a result of this "sign on the dotted line" compromise, the church was left with a newfound definition. Over time, "love" would be slowly morphed into "tolerance" and thereby be mistaken for true virtue.

There was a time not too long ago in our history that this same church knew and practiced those absolutes of truth. This separate entity called "the bride of Christ," knew the endearing terms of this divine affection and she kept her dress clean from the outside infiltrations of the "unclean thing" (see 2 Corinthians 6:17). She was well aware of that slogan of sanctity, penned by that beloved apostle John in his first love-laced letter to his offspring in the faith:

> "Love not the world, neither the things that are in the world. If any man love the world, the love of the Father is not in him." (1 John 2:15)

As the church was faced with this crossroad, something of a very sneaky nature began to transpire. As the definition of **love** began to turn a dismal color of gray, the definition of "**the world**" soon followed suit. The lines became blurred, the boundaries became more obscure, and the result was compromise. Love was no longer an absolute, but now became subject to the ever changing tides of tolerance.

Suddenly, the church woke up one morning and found that the

partner it had shared its bed with was none other than a harlot of a hollow affection. It had left its first love and found itself in the uncharted territory of an affair with another. The world had now insidiously slipped under the covers of this otherwise separated entity called the church, and committed spiritual adultery with it. Surely this indictment from the apostle James would ring desperately true in our day!

> "Ye adulterers and adulteresses, know ye not that the ***friendship of the world*** is enmity with God? Whosoever therefore will be a friend of the world is the enemy of God. (James 4:4)

This perversion of true divine love would permeate throughout the church like a leaven. She would now put her arms around the lover of her choosing and accept all things that God rejects. In the name of "tolerance," her doors would be flung open to an unbridled host of all things sinful.

Inevitably, true repentance from sin was forsaken and transformed into an "everybody's got a vice" mentality. The accountability level dropped below freezing, and the affection of this once spotless bride had frozen over. Now, one would be able to enter her sacred doors, remain in their prefered bondage, and fall headlong in love with her doctrine of tolerance for sin.

The grand scheme had been a success! Satan could now step back and observe with glee that he had accomplished his mission. That mission was to lower the church's standard to the point of a breachable degree. The cracks that now formed in her foundation would be the eventual way into her sacred holy place.

Beloved, let us consider the tragedy of this desensitization of this precious word. The love of God which is spoken of in the Bible is a love unmingled. It does not mix with the recipes of the world because it is an ingredient all its own. To fall in love with Jesus, is to fall in love with His truth. These two inseparable attributes of God, love and truth, will never be parted one from another.

Yes, the Lord fills us with His love for the **SOULS *of the world*** around us, but the **WAYS *of the world***, we must hate. Jesus said it so simply in the book of John, that it leaves no room for private interpretation:

"If you love me, keep my commandments." (John 14:15)

The Lord Jesus was not here on this earth to peddle a message of love that had with it no conditions! Never! What a disgrace He would have been to the Godhead to propose a love that was neither reciprocating nor based on the criteria of heaven. What was the Lord conveying through this verse in John? Was He suggesting a love that was disconnected from devotion? Or, was He implying an affinity that was free of ardent affection? Did He mean to leave the impression that one could simply **"be loved,"** without a supreme and loving surrender back to his Creator?

When He looked at His disciples and made this statement, He knew just exactly what He meant, even if they yet did not know themselves. In this passage, He would use the most pivotal word in all of the Bible: "***IF.***" Oh! How much rides on this little unassuming word! It is the difference between entering into rich communion with God, or staying outside the camp in darkness. All of the word of God hinges upon it!

In the modern era, the church has been duped to believe that this thing called divine love is ***unconditional.*** Everywhere in Christendom you hear it, from pulpit to pew, this oxymoron of these two words being combined: "***Unconditional love.***" However, if we look closer at the words of the Lord Himself in a couple verses later in John 14, we will see quite the opposite implication as opposed to what the modern vernacular would pass off as divine love:

> "He that **HATH** my commandments, and **KEEPETH** them, **HE IT IS** that loveth me: and he that loveth me **SHALL BE LOVED OF MY FATHER**, and *I WILL LOVE HIM*, and will manifest myself to him." (John 14:21)

Oh my! How much is crammed into this passage! We could unpack its sacred truths for hours and yet skim its surface. We see clearly here the criteria of heaven with regards to true divine love. These commandments that God intended for us to **HAVE** and to **KEEP** are nothing less than the reciprocating divine love that is "Shed abroad in our hearts by the Holy Ghost" (see Romans 5:5). The conditions of this love is the **RECEIVING** of the divine life within the heart. To "keep the commandments" is described by the Lord as a sacred adherence to God. This prime mover of all piety called divine love is poured into these earthen vessels as they turn upwards in true gospel obedience to all things truthful.

Repentance is not **JUST** turning from the dirt of one's own degradation, but also turning with open mouth to the heavens to receive the liquid love that "Cometh down from the Father of lights!" (see James 1:17). Obedience to God is not grievous to the consecrated soul that has been filled with this abundant benevolence, rather, it is a delight. I think the apostle John said it so well:

> "For this is the love of God, that we keep His commandments: and His commandments are not grievous." (1 John 5:3)

God's love is indeed *unconditional* on **HIS END**, but it is most utterly *conditional* on **OUR END**! Let us consider the most famous

Bible passage on the planet as an example.

> "For God so **LOVED THE WORLD that HE GAVE** His only begotten Son, that **WHOSOEVER BELIEVES** in Him should not perish, but **RECEIVE** everlasting life." (see John 3:16)

The most important words in this passage, as far as **GOD** is concerned, certainly must be **"*loved*"** and **"*gave*."** The keyword in this passage, as far as **WE** are concerned, is **"*receive.*"**

His infinite love proceeds out of Him as direct as the sunlight lays its brilliant beams upon this otherwise cold planet. Yet, in the winter months all ceases to grow and to produce fruit due to the earth's positional change. This tilt away from the sun is just far enough to deprive it of the necessary nutrients for it to thrive adequately enough for growth. The sunlight is spread out over more of a broad area, rather than in the summer when it concentrates its lofty beams in a more concise manner. The sun is indeed **STILL THERE** producing the same rays, yet the **RECIPIENT** called earth is not in the correct **POSITION** to **RECEIVE** its life-giving force.

We must then, by default, draw the following conclusion about these aforementioned verses. It is the fact that the love of God is a thing that **MUST** be received in order to translate to anything good for our human condition. We cannot simply herald the hollow message of "Jesus loves you" to the mundane masses without a very real bonafide truth being the forerunner to such a statement. That truth is the fact that it was their very own apathy towards their Creator that put Him on that terrible tree of suffering. Our message must always be the same as that prophetic utterance of old from our dear Isaiah:

> "All we like sheep have gone astray; we have turned every one

to his own way; and the LORD hath laid on Him the iniquity of us all." (Isaiah 53:6)

This love that is of God is meaningless to the soul who does not see its own undeserving condition of receiving it. The sinner that is at enmity with his Creator, by default of his own rebellion, should never be told that God "*unconditionally*" loves him. This sort of approach is nothing short of an act of treason toward his very soul. He will never see the need for leaving his state of rebellion if he erroneously believes that there are no conditions upon which he must believe the gospel. Indeed God **DOES** love him. But that is because **GOD is LOVE**, and not because the sinner has something in him that is **LOVABLE**!

Herein lies this great disconnect. That is, that this same sinner must realize by divine illumination, that he is indicted for high treason in the courts of heaven and stands in the state of imminent wrath. Without this knowledge, he knows neither what he is fleeing from, nor what he is actually running to. He has been grossly blinded by the "god of this world" (see 2 Corinthians 4:4) and the veil between himself and the true God is coated with thick layers of delusional apathy. The convincing power of the Holy Ghost has within Himself the unique quality of being able to uncover the heart of anarchy, while simultaneously disclosing that great redemption of Calvary's outstretched hand.

We the church are His mouthpieces and His representatives. As His spokespersons, we are to cooperate with His work in sufficiently preaching the law of God in order to bring about an environment of conviction. By no means can we take up the exclusive work of the Spirit in conviction, but when we speak of His account and indictments towards mankind, it gives the Holy Ghost the ammunition that He can use to slay the tall soldiers of resistance within each human heart. This alone can cause the anarchist of spiritual independence to lay down their arms and surrender to the will of God.

This is the very reason John the baptist had to come as the *forerunner*! As that human megaphone began to preach on those riverbanks (if I may indulge in a bit of a paraphrase here), it likely went a little something like this: "Flee from the wrath to come! Yes, the love of God is about to appear to all men. The approachableness of the living God is about to be unveiled! But, if you want to **RECEIVE** this one, then you must let go of all other lovers in your heart to get it!"

> "Come out from among them, touch not the unclean thing and He will **RECEIVE** you!" (2 Corinthians 6:17)

As we draw this chapter to a close, let us consider the enchantments of this snake oil salesman called Satan. May we cease from buying his watered down versions of healing balms, which he has paraded before the eager Christian in public, whose pockets bulge with the cheap currency of easy-believism. May we cry out for the authentic, the proven, and the time-tested truths of the book of God!

> "Oh Lord, we humbly come before you and ask that you outfit us with a baptism of discernment. May that wisdom that you so readily grant the open-hearted seeker, be poured out without restraint upon this vulnerable, weakened flock, called the modern church. Bring us back to the mount of God where your fire burns with the very passion of your heart, and there, reignite this divine flame within our very bosoms. AMEN"

Chapter 15

# PSYCHOLOGY:
## A BRAINSTORM, OR A BRAINWASH?

*"And my speech and my preaching was not with enticing words of man's wisdom, but in demonstration of the Spirit and of power." 1 Corinthians 2:4*

PAUL THE APOSTLE was a very brilliant man. We know this because of his writings in the New Testament and by the list of accolades he sported in his letter to the Philippians. He leaves no doubt that he was cultivated in the higher religious schools of thought in his day. He could probably line the plaques up on the wall with the best of them. His desk would likely be outfitted with the most elaborate and ornate nameplate, equipped with a most impressive display of letters describing his title among the educated elite.

"Paul A. Apostle, A.B.C.D.E"

You get the picture.

Yet, the unique thing about this man of God is that he would eventually come to lean upon none of these unsure frames. After his glorious conversion, he would readily crumple up his credentials, tear the plaques from his office wall, and chuck it all (along with his name tag) in the dumpster. Yes, he would even come to count those formal notables of nobility as nonsensical, even to the point of giving them the label of **DUNG!** (see Philippians 3). In his interpersonal and celestial interview with the Lord Jesus on his way to Damascus, he would "see the light" and quickly learn his lowly place in the pecking order of God's kingdom. His former title of religious royalty (Pharisee of Pharisees) would quickly be turned into the chiefest of corruptors (see 1 Timothy 1:15) as he gazed upon the brilliance and the nature of all things holy.

Now, let us consider this new ministry of Paul that transpired from this experience. That pharisaical zealot which was once "heady and high-minded" would now understand the dynamics of a newborn kingdom among men. The kingdom that was now in "demonstration of power" would descend into the heart of a man once bent on the very annihilation of the same. Paul would come to know the power of the new birth, which would compel him to flush his formalism and cause him to preach only "Christ and Him crucified."

We now find ourselves some two thousand years removed from Saul's transformation into Paul. As we peek in the back door of this modern institution that the writer of Hebrews called, "The assembly of the firstborn" (see Hebrews 12:23), we find that a very strange mixture has emerged within her back rooms and boardrooms. If we look close enough, with eye salve applied, we will spot a defiling bacteria so insidious that even the very elect can barely spot it. One must look earnestly under a scrutinizing microscope with the very discernment of the Holy Ghost in order to see it. This nearly undetectable microcosm of mutiny has been hidden amidst the stuff in "Achan's tent" (see Joshua 7) for so long, it has been disregarded as impertinent to the bigger picture.

It's highly doubtful that any one person could trace history back to the exact moment that *psychology* made its "Freudian slip" into the house of God. There is no use here at this juncture in our dispensation to try to do so, since it's simply just "water under the bridge" anyhow. I will not attempt to retrace those steps, nor waste ink on the explanation of its own origin and evolution among humankind. All such information is readily accessible online at anyone's fingertips. I will simply point out that psychology's origin **DID NOT** start in the realms of religious thought, nor from a spiritual origin in any sense of the word. No, this anecdotal anomaly of *"mind science"* came directly out of the same, that is, from the *science of man's mind.*

When the advent of the "low self-esteem" model began to crossbreed with the gospel, a spiritual crime of the highest order was committed. The selfless gospel of Jesus Christ came under the assault of a perpetrator of a most insidious nature. This concept that mankind's ills could be traced to a "low opinion of himself" somehow made its way through the back door of the church, slipped up the aisle, and set quietly down among the faithful. Conversely, the Bible teaches that mankind's problem is that he thinks too **HIGHLY** of himself. Although Paul would tell the church at Philippi to: "Let nothing be done through strife or vainglory; but in lowliness of mind let each ***esteem each other better than themselves***"(Philippians 2:3), we have somehow been sold the opposite bill of goods from the mental health community.

I'm certain that the rich young ruler in which Jesus lovingly showed his shortcomings to (see Mathew 19:16-29), would have walked away with head hung low under the straining conviction of the Lord's words. Nowadays however, we would take him aside, calm his fears with a shot of self-motivation, and polish his ego with a statement something like this: "Now, I know He chided you a bit, even said you weren't a good person, but you're really not that bad of a guy. What you really need after such a wounding is a reaffirmation of your self-worth."

Bear with me a moment as I attempt to explain how "low self-esteem" is actually just pride in reverse. When an individual feels inferior to their peers, maybe even driving them to the point of introversion, they are engaging in an insidious form of pride. That said soul has an opinion of itself that feels **cheated** out of their **deserved** attention. Feeling that they are owed more than what they are receiving, they take on a reversed form of pride that manifests in a severe form of neediness. Becoming overly needy of acknowledgement from their peers, while at the same time not getting those same needs fulfilled, they revert instead into a darkness of self-sufficiency and independence of the highest order. They become utterly obsessed with their own attention. It is here that they seemingly become untouchable, introverted, and exhibit this perceived "low self-esteem." But on the contrary, they are simply manifesting pride in reverse. Their real problem is that they think too highly of themselves and expect humanity to pacify that great self concern within. Their disappointment stems from an over expectation, and an underrated supply of attention. It is simply pride, cloaked in "low self esteem."

The gospel experience destroys this need from within, abolishes the pride, and grants the contentment of being an adoptive child of God. The need to look outside (or even inside) of oneself for completeness, melts away into oblivion in light of the divine "Love shed abroad in the heart by the Holy Ghost" (see Romans 5:5).

The very purpose that Satan penetrated the sacred halls of the church with such a notion of low self-esteem was clearly to eliminate man's responsibility for his own sin. If he can divert the ownership of man's indescrepencies away from himself and project his infractions upon his environment, his raising, or his peers, then he has successfully removed the need for heart repentance. We cannot blame our sins, no matter what our environment may be, on anything but our own wicked hearts. Consider this passage in the book of James as proof of the same:

> "But every man is tempted, when he is drawn away of **HIS OWN** lust, and enticed." (James 1:14)

I often hear in church circles such statements as: "You have to love yourself, before you can love others." This concept is none other than a product of psychology's infiltration into the sacred body of Christ. When dealing with this problem of "low self-love," let us consider this passage in the book of Matthew to see how Jesus Himself deals with it in light of the demands of the gospel:

> "Then said Jesus unto His disciples, If any *man* will come after me, let him **DENY HIMSELF,** and take up his cross, and follow me. (Matthew 16:24)

And another,

> "If any *man* come to me, and **HATE** not his father, and mother, and wife, and children, and brethren, and sisters, yea, **AND HIS OWN LIFE ALSO**, he cannot be my disciple." (Luke 14:26)

If Jesus is here telling us to "deny ourselves," and to "hate our own lives also," how can we then draw the conclusion that He is suggesting that we humans possess a low self-esteem? It becomes utterly clear that the Lord is showing us the **TRUE** nature of our problem as human beings, **THE LOVE OF SELF**! No! Not an underestimated love for ourselves, but an overinflated adoration of our own person above our fellow man! This is what causes the drunkard to lose consideration for all other lives besides his own. This is what causes the adulterer to pay no regards to marital contracts. This is what causes the thief to take what is not lawfully his. Sin! Selfishness! Self rule! Hedonism! Praise God that the gospel cures all of this. It drives the selfish ambitions of the heart down into the grave, promotes the loss of our own lives in servitude, and abolishes the need for the pleasing of ourselves.

The gospel of Jesus Christ is a mighty powerful thing. It employs the direct agency of God's divine influence upon the heart and mind by opening the inner eyes of mankind and exposing him to that divinity. "The eyes of your understanding being enlightened; that ye may know what is the hope of His calling, and what the riches of the glory of His inheritance in the saints" (Ephesians 1:18). It is an **EXTERNAL** divine force affecting an **INTERIOR** condition.

The complexity of man's sin, and his anarchic disconnect from the Creator, call for such an exposure to come from beyond the boundaries of his own depraved heart. When the heavenly kingdom meets the human condition, all the mental faculties are suspended and God is able to penetrate that mighty fortress of intellectual fortitude within us. In order to slay him and strip him of all his weapons of self-righteousness, He reveals Himself to the degree that is necessary to produce those humiliating results. We only need to revisit the many accounts in the Bible to see this penetrating principle in such subjects as Daniel (Daniel 10:8), Isaiah (Isaiah 6:5), Paul (Acts 9:3), and John (Revelation 1:17), for example.

The reason that this ***self-contained*** model called psychology is so flawed, is because it is just that, ***contained within ourselves.*** It is also the very reason it cannot be mingled with the power of the gospel. This unhealthy mixture of human ingenuity with spiritual simplicity cannot mix anymore than can oil and water. The word of God is very clear in regards to the bottomless, unsearchable depravity of man's heart. Jeremiah would belt out such a proclamation in the 17th chapter with this declaration of degradation:

> "The heart *is* deceitful above all *things*, and desperately wicked: **who can know it?**" (Jeremiah 17:9)

He then answers the very question with the next verse, proclaiming the exclusive claims of God's possession of the keys to the chambers of that same wicked heart:

> "I the LORD search the heart, *I* try the reins, even to give every man according to his ways, *and* according to the fruit of his doings." (Jeremiah 17:10)

To call upon man, in order to fix man, is an exercise in futility. We could liken such an endeavor to two side by side ships on fire in the ocean, trying to put out their flames with common fire extinguishers. Even if one is in worse condition, and further involved in flames than the other, such instruments do not have the adequate supply of chemical resources to put out either fire. Even if the ship with the **lesser** fire should direct all its resources on the one farther along in its burning, it would prove to be futile. Certainly, one may be in better condition than the other, but even in its better condition, it could not save itself nor the more involved one. Their only course of action is to call upon a rescuer of a higher order and abandon their ships.

In 2 Corinthians, we can clearly see Paul's **version** of psychology. We can, by comparison, make the assessment that his approach to the **science of the mind** has a far weightier implication than our modern conceptions of it. I will relate the said verse with the Greek definitions beside key words to show the point I wish to convey:

> "For the weapons of our warfare *are* not carnal (behavior which is typical of **human nature**), but mighty through God to the pulling down of strongholds (a fortress) casting down (forcibly yank down), imaginations (reasonings), and every high thing (that which is lifted up) that exalteth (I raise, lift up) itself against the knowledge (a knowing) of God, and bringing into captivity every thought to the obedience of Christ." (2 Corinthians 10:4-5)

If we were to paraphrase those verses and make them a little more relative to today's vernacular, I believe they would look something like this:

> "For the weapons of our warfare *are* not found in **behavioral modification,** but mighty through God to the pulling down of **our fortified will**, yanking down **human reason** which lifts itself up and tries to **usurp itself over** our 'hearts cry' to **know God.** We subdue every thought and subject them to **the nature of Christ** and His loving obedience to the Father."

Again, this is only my compilation based on the Greek definition. I certainly do not want to alter the original text, but I think we can see by bringing out these definitions, just what the apostles' intentions were. It certainly becomes obvious to me that Paul was here declaring that the resources within man himself are inadequate. Being of that high minded satanic nature, our own minds can never be called upon as an adequate resource to cure itself, let alone its peers. The phrase, "But mighty through God" would certainly have to draw the distinction between the divine capabilities of God, and the futile efforts from within ourselves to conquer the stronghold of that fortress called human reason.

The apostle also knew by experience that the mental faculties of man could not be repaired by virtue of reasoning, resolve, or any form of self-restraint. No, he knew there had to be a transformation of the spirit of man, via receiving a new heart. In Romans chapter 12, Paul makes a direct statement to the necessity of this renewing:

> "And be not conformed to this world: but be ye **transformed** by the **renewing** of your mind, that ye may prove what *is* that good, and acceptable, and perfect, will of God." (Romans 12:2)

I love this Greek definition for the word "transformed," as used here:

> "properly, transformed *after being with; transfigured*."
> (Source: Bible Hub/Strongs # 3339)

It simply implies the metamorphosis that takes place when the Son of God enters His temple of the human heart. A new creature emerges by divine effect of the indwelling Christ! Subsequently, the word "renewing" follows close behind as a good clean up batter:

> "properly, *a new development; a renewal, achieved by God's power.*" (source:Bible Hub/ Strongs #342)

This mind renewal is the inevitable result of the Spirit of the living God washing out the old life and filling the heart with His word and His nature. Man needs a new heart, hands down. This is the only remedy and actual *fix* for his depraved nature.

When I was a young boy, my brother and I would often try to dam up our little local stream with mounds mixed with clay and mud. We would dig the stock out of the side of the bank next to the water and create large dams across the creek (large for our little world at least). We were often successful in producing an adequate barricade to hold back a fair amount of water. However, as the water kept flowing in, soon the creek/pond would swell beyond capacity and eventually spill over the dam, washing the clay barrier away. We simply could not contain it but for a short time, and just as water always does, it found its way around the barricade and eventually breached our little project. We felt very powerful in the fact that we could control the amount of the water going down the stream. Nevertheless, much to our dismay, we would lose our work and watch the murky, clay-colored water wash down the creek again.

This illustration is a perfect depiction of man trying to stop the flow of that inner flood, which is sin that proceeds out of the heart. Yes, you may try to dam it up, and you may even try to redirect it with medications, treatments, and suggestive reasoning. Yet inevitably, just like the water in that little creek, over the course of time, it will always find its way to the place in which it was intended to go. The Word of God proclaims that a "spirit of disobedience" (see Ephesians 2:2) dwells within every unregenerate individual, and those who are "in the flesh" (see Romans 8:8) cannot please God. Neither can we self-willed beasts produce anything of divine love from within our own defiled heart. Although we may be able to perform outward duties of philanthropic actions, we simply cannot produce moral excellence. Tweak them as we may, given the right set of circumstances, we will ultimately vomit forth the torrents of rebellion that hide within our very own bosoms. This is precisely why we must be given a **NEW** heart in regeneration (see

## PSYCHOLOGY: A BRAINSTORM, OR A BRAINWASH?

Ezekiel 36:26).

The soul of man is like a runaway train and is steeped in disobedience. It has indeed gone its "***own way***" (see Isaiah 53:6) on a path of unbridled anarchy. This locomotive called ***self-will*** only knows but one course, that is the one straight ahead of it. Its conductor, passed out at the controls and oblivious to his own demise, has not the wherewithal to put the brakes to it. The path of this soul train is uninhibited by any deterrent that would seek to impede its progress. This is why the Bible speaks of the "saving of the soul" (see Hebrews 10:39). It must literally be saved from its own self-destruction. This train can only be stopped by way of coming to the end of the tracks! It is of no use to throw continual debris in front of it in order to impair it or stop its progress. It is a train, and its weightiness affords it its own path down the mountainside.

Likewise, we cannot possibly contain the soul of man by mere study, observation, or fruitless redirection. It is the very "spirit of disobedience" (see Ephesians 2:2), and it cannot possibly be tamed by the "***whip and chair***" of human resources. It must be allowed to come to the end of itself. The inertia of the train can only be stopped by virtue of its own wreckage.

When a human soul is finally done with its own reckless gig, it is then, and only then, that it will submit itself to a more steady conductor. Only the Lord Jesus Christ can clean up such wreckage. He alone can place the train back on the tracks and provide it with the new conductor (i.e. Himself). He alone can navigate it properly through the woes and treacheries of the tracks that lie ahead. The distinctive difference between man's ways and God's ways, is that one is simply a ***treatment***, and the other is a ***cure***. To try and redirect the psyche of man to perform benevolent behavior to the betterment of himself and society, is indeed an exercise in futility. Without the transforming power of the Holy Ghost and the efficacy of the blood of Christ to wash away that dirty conscience, there is no hope for true bonafide change. Only He can provide that new heart with a sustaining power to overcome itself.

We cannot hope to live out the fairy tale that we can somehow change the heart of man through therapeutic methodologies. He may indeed change **some** of his outward appearances and actions through a change in his behavior and we may even be able to "numb him up" to his surroundings. We may even be able to impede him on his impending path to self-destruction with programs and prescriptions, but we will never cure the rottenness of this inner fruit with anything short of the power of the new birth. Man simply cannot be changed by man. He must have a power encounter, he must experience regeneration, and he must leave off his old putrid life. This is the only hope that he has for true inner transformation:

- "Give us help from trouble: for vain *is* the help of man." (Psalms 108:12)

- "Through God we shall do valiantly: for He *it is that* shall tread down our enemies." (Psalm 108:13)

- "For it is God which worketh in you both to will and to do of *His* good pleasure." (Philippians 2:13)

Chapter 16

# ETERNAL SECURITY:
## FAVORITISM OR FARCE?

*"Keep yourselves in the love of God, looking for the mercy of our Lord Jesus Christ unto eternal life." Jude 1:21*

*"Take heed, brethren, lest there be in any of you an evil heart of unbelief, in departing from the living God." Hebrews 3:12*

IF I WERE FORCED TO CHOOSE A DOCTRINE, one that I believe has had the greatest effect on the modern church, I would have to select the doctrine of "Calvinism." It has come to be known in Christian circles by a few different titles, such as, "Once saved, always saved" (OSAS for short), "Eternal security," and "Reformed theology," to name a few. This doctrine is so subtle and insidious that most don't even realize that this ghostly "apparition of apathy" haunts their very own spiritual lifestyles. It has subtly encroached upon the overall preaching of the gospel in the last five hundred years, even to the point of reaching into the staunchest sectors of it.

The 5 points of Calvinism, or T.U.L.I.P, as it has come to be abbreviated by, was a flower grown in the greenhouse of the post-reformation era. This theological model was a brainchild of a man named John Calvin. Although this doctrine has its actual beginning in the 5th century through the pen of St. Augustine of Hippo, Calvin would be the one to chisel its sculpture into "a form of godliness" for all to gaze upon as a finished bust. Calvins particular finished prototype, would no doubt be a by-product of his attempt to escape from the religious tyranny of institutionalized religion. Being a breakaway of the great "Roman mother," as was Luther, Calvin would build on Luther's "justification by faith alone" model, and would be a key figure in the Reformation during the 1500's.

Although his actual conversion account is a bit sketchy and ambiguous, we are not here to bash the man, nor to question his personal piety. I have no interest in Calvins personal accolades, whether good or bad. Anyone can find plenty of history on Mr. Calvin with a click of a button, and can easily wade through the historical account to make their own judgments. Our focus here is on the **effects** of the doctrine upon the church of Jesus Christ. We are also not here to attempt to delve into the **doctrine** as a **whole** and to break all the theology down in a systematic fashion by combing through the fine hairs of its structure and searching out all its microscopic parasites. I have been trying to avoid bogging this book down with exegetical exactitudes and doctrinal dogma, and I hope to continue to do so.

I am certain I could easily call upon 50 verses (like the 2 irrefutable ones at our chapter heading) rather quickly in order to refute the doctrine of **eternal security** and sink its vessel mercilessly to the bottom of the sea. However, I have found in my experience that those staunch supporters of this doctrine have their feet rather set in concrete and have become more unmovable than the "Rock of Gibraltar." So, it is not my intention to convince such people to change their theology, although that would be a pleasant fruit of this labor, nonetheless.

My intention here is not so much to talk about **what** the doctrine is, but rather, **why** it is even in existence. Or, in other words, what is the **reason** it is believed by the holders of it? Some may not even realize **why** they are believing it and hopefully this little attempt to expose its subtle nature may enlighten them to this reality. All doctrines that have been "spun off" of the original biblical text, have their origin in something either latently nefarious, or overtly edifying. If one does not investigate the **origin** of a thing in which they place their trust in, then they might as well book the next flight on a jetliner that has been manufactured by toddlers.

What I see here with this doctrine, more than anything, is what I call a case of "Pendulum Syndrome." I have witnessed this sort of thing so many times in my own generation to know that this is a very real spiritual malady. When folks come out of doctrinal bondage, they tend to go full steam ahead in the opposite direction. I have watched people come out of "legalism" and head straight forward into "liberalism." Conversely, I have witnessed folks come out of being **liberated** by the Spirit, and dive head first into **legal** quicksand, then struggle to get free "while being yet in the flesh" (see Romans 7:5).

This **virus of the spirit** is hard to kick when one keeps going into the same doctor's office for treatment, that is to say, one that is full of patients that are afflicted with the same virus as themselves. The infection rate is exponential, due to being exposed to those who suffer from the same sickness and where variants are always churning up new ways to get into your system. A church that is **sick** with a false doctrine is just like that doctors office with its hackers and sneezers. They are constantly filling the air with droplets of the very thing they are there to be treated for.

When one breaks free from doctrinal error, the pendulum automatically swings the other way, and many times, there is no one there to stop it. Almost inevitably, that poor soul fails to settle down in the happy medium between **law** and **grace**. There is indeed such a **place**, but one must be willing to apply the eye salve of objectivity to see it. I have witnessed such blindness from this "syndrome," that it leaves me astonished at its very defiance to logic itself, let alone its doctrinal fallacy. I have many times laid very plain and logical explanations before such people with great loving earnestness, only to see a shrugged reaction. I quickly found that they have painted themselves into a corner of some sort of absolute and the only way for them to get out is to walk through the wet paint of their own pride.

It is just my hunch that Mr. Calvin likely suffered from "Pendulum Syndrome" as well. When he came out of the **Babylonian** church model called the **Catholic Church** after hearing the cry of the Spirit to "Come out of her my people," he likely tripped at the threshold of her jeweled doorway and fell headlong into a liberal ideology of sorts. Although some would argue that this doctrine is anything but liberal with its thesis on the **Perseverance of the Saints,** its insidious effect is a complacency hidden beneath the surface. When Mr. Calvin (who was no doubt a brilliant theologian in some respects) broke free of the Catholic Church and its *works salvation* mentality, he simply went too far the other way.

You may ask, what is the harm in believing such a doctrine? One that basically says: God purchases us, seals us with eternal seal, holds us in his hand, and lets nothing separate from His love? Indeed, this all sounds like a most lovely set up for the gospel experience! Fitted with all provisions of a security, eternally purchased with blood! One that cannot be altered in any wise! One that, no matter the position of the creature, whether in faithfulness or folly, he is held by the unseen hands of parental providence! What a plan, what a deal, and what a blessing!

The only problem with this wonderful "entree of gospel goodies," is that it just simply doesn't work for **GOD**. Although this doctrine is impressive with its palatable plate of dogmatic dainties, it is simply not a meal that God has prepared for mankind. The problem with this whole ideology is not that it doesn't work good for **man**, oh, it works for **his fleshly desires** quite well indeed. The issue at hand is **how** it makes ***God look,*** in spite of how comfortable it may make ***man feel.***

In the book of Acts, we get a wee glimpse of the nature of God and His character concerning His dealings with the sons and daughters of men. In chapter 17, we have Paul's great sermon at Athens resounding from Mars Hill, verbally tearing down the altars of all other gods, even to the point of finding a parking place for the Most High in the empty slot called "TO THE UNKNOWN GOD" (vs. 23). He would show them the essence of Jehovah God and His entreating nature by painting Him as a good God that loves the pursuit of Himself by His creatures!

> "And hath made of one blood all nations of men for to dwell on all the face of the earth, and hath determined the times before appointed, and the bounds of their habitation; That they should seek the Lord, ***if haply they might feel after Him***, and find Him, though He be not far from every one of us." (Acts 17:27)

"If haply (perhaps) **THEY** may **FEEL** after **HIM**." Oh, do you see it? God loves the pursuit of His heart by His creatures. How wonderful a notion it is, that He somehow leaves us in our various and sundry locations within this planet and yet allows us the privilege to seek Him, and to see Him, even within the very handiwork of His creation. Paul would again echo this same sentiment in the great book of Romans:

> "For the invisible things of Him from the creation of the world ***are clearly seen,*** being understood by the things that are made, *even* His eternal power and Godhead; so that they are without excuse." (Romans 1:20)

Imagine a God that would **select** His subjects that **He wishes** to worship Him! How narcissistic a notion! My friends, think of this in the natural course of our own lives as human beings. Do we not all feel that **Communism,** in its forced hommage, is in fact **a tyranny**? Are we then accusing God of "spiritual communism" to say that He seals us up within His celestial borders, never to possess the beauty of choice?! Oh, not even the angels could accept such a notion! "**LET** all the angels of God worship Him" (Hebrews 1:6). Imagine if it were written thusly: "**MAKE** all the angels of God worship Him." Why, surely we would accuse Him of being a divine dictator, and certainly, we would have such a right to do so.

Indeed it is no doubt true that God selects **certain folks** for **certain tasks.** "Many are **called**, but few are **chosen**"(Mathew 22:14). Lets say for example, when it comes to Pauls momentous task of taking the gospel to the Gentile world, he was indeed **CHOSEN** on the basis of Gods foreknowledge. However, it was based on his **FAITHFULNESS** to carry it through to completion, and not simply an arbitrary decision on the part of God."

> "And I thank Christ Jesus our Lord, who hath enabled me, for that He **counted me faithful**, putting me into the ministry." (1 Timothy 1:12)

Could the Lord have entrusted such a mission to a quitter? Would you and I have the benefits that we now have and enjoy from his labors? Could we be basking in the light of such truth, and have the access to the wealth of knowledge and instruction in the New Covenant without a faithful Paul at the helm of this ever imperative transition? I think the answer is clear. So certainly we see why (the few) are **chosen for service**, while the whole world (the many) are **called to salvation**! Let us turn back to Acts 17 to reiterate this point with a punctuation mark! It is the undeniable fact that God has made available to **ALL OF MANKIND,** this wonderful gift of salvation!

> "And the times of this ignorance God winked at; but now commandeth ***ALL MEN everywhere to repent.***" (Acts 17:30)

The problem with the "Doctrine of election" is that it paints a stingy little picture of a God who arbitrarily picks His own admirers from the sea of humanity. He would then need to "fence them in" as one would pen up an unruly dog in order to keep them faithful to their property boundaries. If there were no opportunity to falter in our love for God, it would hold no value between Creator and creature. This liberal license of eternal security is indeed a wet blanket on the flames of divinely reciprocated love. If the passion passes not from heart flame to heart flame on the sheer basis of love, then it has but "tinkling brass and clanging cymbals" as the instruments to play at its very own wedding feast.

Some may raise the objection here that for us to be able to ***choose salvation*** ourselves would negate the very sovereignty of God. One may object, "Does not Jesus Himself state, 'And I give unto them eternal life; and they shall never perish, neither shall any man pluck them out of my hand' (John 10:28)?"

To adequately answer that objection, I must share a little account of a situation I had with a nest of baby birds a few years ago. I found this downed bird nest under the deck of my house after it had fallen from somewhere within the rafters above. This is a deck that one can walk under as it extends from the upper floor of a raised ranch style house. My thought was to restore the nest to the safety of the rafters and give them a new chance for survival. These were birds far too young to be out in the world on their own just yet. I was able to locate the fledglings running about on the ground trying to hide from the perceived monster that was now trying to save them. I was able to subdue one of the fledglings and scoop it up in my hands. I cuffed my hand in the same manner you might do when getting a drink from a stream and this afforded it a warm safe place. However, the youngster didn't see this rescue the same way as I did and bailed over the safe walls I had created for it with my very hands. It found itself upon the ground once again and ran quickly into the adjacent woods. Due to the thickness of the underbrush, I could not recover it. Of course the mother was squawking violently from a nearby branch, which added to its panic, no doubt.

Now, I did **all that I could** to restore the fledgling to the comforts of its own nest. However, due to fear, distrust, and confusion of circumstances, it left out of its safe abode and took its chances upon the ground. Its opportunity of survival exponentially dropped to likely around zero as it fled into the abyss of predation and starvation. It wasn't that this little bird had **no safe walls** around it that put it in danger and caused it to be **unsaved**, rather, it was the fact that it **arbitrarily decided** to bail from the safety of its **rescuer**.

Like myself and that little bird, God will indeed hold us in His hand **as long** as we are locked in there by faith and full trust of heart. But, the moment that we decide to scale the walls and leap to the ground, His hands are just as tied as mine was with the little fledgling. The fact that God has granted us free will, ties His very hands and prevents Him from overriding the decision for us to bail out.

When Jesus said that "no man can pluck you out of my hand," He was simply alluding to the fact that there are no **outside circumstances** that can simply waltz up to us, grab us by the hand, and jerk us out from God's protective nest. Even Paul, in his list of **outside sources** in the book of Romans (a list of things that could never separate us from God's love), never referred to *ourselves, or our own hearts,* in the equation. He rather listed all the things *outside of our* experience as inadequate to drive the wedge in between us and God. He sums it all up in the words "Nor any *other creature,* shall be able to separate us from the love of God, which is in Christ Jesus our Lord" (Romans 8:35-39).

Every impenetrable fortress is secured from *the inside.* A citadel is fortified from within, so as not to be penetrated by outside infiltrators. If a person on the outside tries to get in, they will be prevented by the security measures that are in place, whether it be locks, iron doors, security guards, etc. However, if an assailant were to stand outside to entice and convince the folks within the safety of the walls that they are no longer hostile and have had a change of heart, this could open the door for negotiations. The potential victims within the citadel may possibly be convinced of the amicable nature of the assailant, unlock the door, remove the bars, and venture out for the promised truce.

The choice is made from the *inside of a thing* when it comes to the kingdom of God as well. If it were not so, then it would simply be considered a *Communist prison,* and not a *Theocratic fortress.* This is why the apostle Jude would say "**KEEP YOURSELVES IN**, *the love of God*" (Jude 1:21). It is our free-will choice to stay inside the mighty fortress of His love. Indeed, great and wonderful provisions are there in the Spirit to enable us to resist the encroaching enemies against our souls who would beckon us back outside, but we must *abide inside* if we are to be recipients of those protective conditions.

One of the dangers of Calvinism is that it places God's sovereignty *over* His very nature. For example, the Lord has made this declaration in His word:

"Come. And let him that is athirst come. And ***whoseover will***, ***let him take*** the water of life freely." (Revelation 22:17)

Oh, do we not see it? How could a sovereign God go against His own policies that He has put in place? His own natural benevolence would prevent Him from changing ***any*** of His revealed promises. Suppose one day the Lord would wake up "grumpy" and make this declaration:

"I know that I have previously said: '***Whosoever will,*** let him come and drink,' and yes, that is chiseled in stone, but today I'm feeling a bit under the weather and not in the best of moods. Therefore, since I am ***sovereign,*** I'm going to change the stipulations of this verse, and add a new clause therein. Instead of simply: (***whosoever will***), I am going to insert an 'I' in the equation and alter it to 'Whosoever (***I) will,*** let him come.' I'm in the mood to pick and choose today, so I'm not letting this out to ***all*** of my creatures, but instead only a selected few. I know my book says I am not a 'respecter of persons,' but today, I'm just not feeling my typical self, and wish to choose my subjects for my ***own personal*** worship needs. After all, I'm feeling a bit narcissistic today and with the mood I'm in, I'm searching for a certain class of admirers."

Imagine this! Would not the whole of the universe scream against such injustice and partiality? Would not God be accused of being a dictator and a tyrant, even a control freak? Indeed He would be scoffed at by all the heavenly hosts! To say that His sovereignty trumps His very nature, is a contradiction of terms. He is ***immutable*** (unchanging), and what He has said, He has said. Yes, He indeed says "I will have mercy upon whom I will have mercy" (see Romans 9:15), but that statement can only be understood in the light of what He has *already* put in place as a divine, eternal principle. "He **WILL have** all men to be saved" (see 1 Timothy 2:4), and He is simply not going to oppose His own will.

If the Lord were to go back on His own word, it would cause Him to cease from being the very Sovereign God that He Himself makes claims of. "For You have magnified *your word* above all *your name*" (see Psalm 138:2). God indeed has the power to *do anything* at any time, but He does *not always* exercise this power because of His commitment to His very own personal integrity. It is simply because His own nature prevents Him from breaking the essence of who He is. Oh, I am so glad for His immutability!

Imagine a divine entity who acted out of nothing but irrational emotional swings! Think of a whimsical sovereign with no self-restraint! We should indeed recoil at the thought of this! He has set certain things in stone and He will not touch them, simply because they are a reflection of His benevolence and long-suffering toward His creature. He is "Not willing *that any* should perish, but that *all should come* to repentance" (2 Peter 3:9). Oh, this is the reason He has kept back from cracking the sky with His very showing! Sovereignty! Oh, yes indeed, and that sovereignty is being exercised in the fact that He *chooses* not to smoke this earth with the fire of His judgment before He has given all creatures the *opportunity to hear* His good news. "And this gospel of the kingdom will be preached in all the world as a witness to all the nations, and then the end will come" (Mathew 24:14).

One may also make the objection, based on Jesus' words in the Gospel of John, that a man cannot make any move towards God except by divine will. "No man can come to me, except the Father which hath sent me, *draw him*: and I will raise him up at the last day" (John 6:44).

But, just exactly what does this infer? Does it mean that man has no inquisition whatsoever concerning God, except there be some kind of divine vacuum that pulls him into the very presence of God? Or, is there something much deeper and more profound here? Jesus would later tell the disciples, "And, if I be lifted up from the earth, will **draw all men** unto me " (John 12:32). How is it that the Lord being elevated on the cross is able to draw **all men**? This word "**draw**" used here is the same Greek word used in the above verse in John 6. Let's look at the definition:

> "properly, induce (draw in), focusing on the **attraction-power involved with the drawing.**"(source Bible Hub/ Strongs #1670)

Indeed, the Lord Jesus "lifted up" is an **attraction** to the sinner when they have been convinced of their sin by the enhancement of the Holy Ghost, and have seen their **need** for redemption. Nevertheless, "the drawing of all men" is an allusion to the fact that it is **available for all to look upon and live!**

Paul would make the statement to the Galatians that "Jesus Christ has been evidently set forth crucified among you" (see Galatians 3:1). Meaning, that the cross was indeed an evident **historical fact** that had taken place and that the grace of God had now provided a way out for **all men**, "For the grace of God that bringeth salvation hath appeared **to all men**" (Titus 2:11).

And, as we alluded to earlier, nature itself testifies to the very existence of God, and yet, has within itself no intrinsic drawing power. However, it can invoke **within us** an **inquisition** that would allow one to ask questions such as these: "Who made all of this? Is there something behind it? Am I just here on this earth to enjoy this nature, and simply live and die?" These questions arise out of the creature because

God "Hath set the world (eternity) in their heart, so that no man can find out the work that God maketh from the beginning to the end" (Ecclesiastes 3:11). The very inquisition of man's nature links him to the Creator. He has within him the residue of that first garden experience and the searching echoes of the Creator calling, "Adam where are you?" When God turns His ear toward the earth, He is always looking for "first responders." They are those who have perked up their own spiritual antenna and sent forth the deep cry of "inner inquisition" as a signal to the heavens.

> "Deep calleth unto deep at the noise of thy waterspouts: all thy waves and thy billows are gone over me." (Psalms 42:7)

The Lord is ever searching for the signal of a response, emitting from man, as well as man is looking for one from Him. He indeed sends out the faint signal to all men everywhere, "For the eyes of the LORD run to and fro throughout the whole earth, to shew Himself strong in the behalf of *them* whose heart *is* perfect toward Him" (2 Chronicles 16:9). No matter the exact origin, whether from within man, or outside of man, it is all one in the same. The whole purpose is for **RECONCILIATION**! To sit around and haggle over the question, "Which is first, the chicken or the egg?" is to cheat man and God out of precious time they could be enjoying together. Let us move on from the debate of the *signal origin*, and focus on the "communion of the union." In one way or another, ***all things*** **do** come ***from Him,*** and do go ***back to Him,*** including our very own free will. Yet still, that most coveted and most precious commodity from our sovereign God, is indeed that wonderful free will of man. It shall never be meddled with, for if it were to happen, it would be defiled most atrociously.

I have heard countless accounts of people simply asking a question in their mind while sitting on a mountain top, sitting by a river, or just wandering through the woods. They had the thought: "I wonder what is behind all this?" Suddenly, God spoke to them. He then guided them into a place where they could be "expounded the way of God more perfectly" (see Acts 18:26) and as a result, they were able to eventually be converted. So that *"drawing"* is composed of many different factors and we should never limit Him to any **one way** in which that interest for Himself be sparked in the human heart. Evidence of His person is all around us, and all of nature testifies to the beauty and creating powers of the God of the heavens. He will **always** get us to Jesus and the cross, if and when our heart is open to hear His voice.

Indeed there are moments when the drawing power is increased by individuals coming into a revival setting or an assembly where the Spirit of God is moving and **enhanced**. These drawings may increase, or they may wane, but nevertheless they will always be there in some capacity or another. Otherwise men would have an excuse to ignore such a beautiful Creator. Nevertheless, because of the testimony of God all around them, every man is without excuse as to whether they should pursue their Creator or not.

So, the drawing is at least twofold, and can perhaps even be a threefold thing: The testimony of nature, the evidence of the cross, and the divine influence of the Holy Ghost upon the heart. The latter 2 of these are absolutely necessary for ultimate conversion, but there are more ways than one to get us within the earshot of God's voice. If you wanted to, you could even toss a fourth drawing by mentioning adversity and human suffering. Many times these are also catalysts of humility that can cause the soul to cry out to a power higher than themselves.

God will simply never defile the free will of His creature, but He will indeed put great pressures upon it. Yet, He will never turn it one way or the other; it is the **influence** that affects the decision and not the ***sovereignty*** of God. Again, to make God's sovereignty the prime mover in this situation, is to indeed make Him a tyrant. It makes Him appear as if He owns an earth size "toy soldier set." One that He simply likes playing with and moving the pieces around to engage in battles, as He sees fit for His own entertainment. It is an insult to call Him thus. However, He has indeed put the creature in a ***place of great void***, so that they may "perhaps, feel after Him."

A grace that is ***irresistible*** is no grace at all. The very essence of grace, being the divine influence on the heart, cannot produce the final result of choice. This is left alone in the hands of the creature. Although God's great influence can take one to the pinnacle of conversion, it can in no wise tamper with this wonderful gift of choice. In the great book of Acts we see such an account. A man of great ***worldly influence***, comes under the ***influence divine*** to the point of a ***near*** bend of his will and knee to the Most High God. Albeit much pressure was applied to his stubborn will, this mighty conviction was still insufficient to break the will of a king. Paul, while in bonds and under the scrutiny of false accusations by the Jews, would be allowed by this king to speak on his own behalf. Paul would, as his manner was, take advantage of the moment and give his conversion testimony in front of the nobles. In light of his lengthy discourse before the courts of royalty, he would ask this King Agrippa a question. King Agrippa's response would be telling of a man on the brink of decision, yet ***not quite willing*** to make the great leap of faith.

> "King Agrippa, believest thou the prophets? I know that thou believest. Then Agrippa said unto Paul, ***Almost thou persuadest me to be a Christian.*** And Paul said, I would to God, that not only thou, ***but also all that hear me this day***, were both almost, and altogether such as I am, except these bonds." (Acts 26: 27-29)

Oh, the pursuit of God after the heart of man can seem relentless! Conversely, the stubbornness of the human can be equal to the task. Many souls have been bent under the mighty wind of the forces of His love and persuasion. Yet, these mighty oaks stand with roots dug too deep within the commitment of their own pride in order for them to be broken. I have witnessed many go out of this life in such a state. Even with God's great persuasive torrents of convincing power upon their old, cold, dead heart, they remain steadfast in their commitment to their own ways.

I believe God's most beautiful creation out of everything that He has made, is the simple free will of His creatures. Oh the risk of this! The possibilities of mutiny are endless and indeed have played out even among the angels themselves. Who, by the way, were formed within the very presence of such a benevolent being. Nonetheless, they bailed out of His perfect will in order to usurp Him and start their own **spiritual coup** (see Jude 1:6). It simply shows the wisdom and the humility of God to be able to create creatures in such a way to be able to step back from them, and say something like this:

> "If you should choose me, or choose me not, I am still going to create you. I'm still going to take the risk that you will run completely the other way, but this is a risk I'm willing to take because I cannot enjoy our communion except it be challenged by the opposite effect."

Is it not evident in the original garden that God loves the element of choice? Did not the forbidden fruit represent this? That "tree of the knowledge of good and evil" represents a risk by God that is unfathomable to the human mindset. When a child finds a small, perceivably abandoned paddling of ducklings, their little mind goes into rescue mode. The first thing they do is run to the garage, grab the nearest box and facilitate the orphans by containing them within 4 walls. Not so with God! He has allowed man to navigate through the perils of an earth that has been largely disconnected from Himself, hoping that he will seek the origin of this kind Creator that has hatched him forth from the image of His very own person.

Again, the Lord's risk here with this thing called free-will choice was enormous. Throw in a beguiling reptile and you have the odds stacked against Himself from the git go. But, this is just how confident He is in the expression of **HIMSELF**, and not in the faithfulness of man. His willingness to "subject the creature to vanity" (see Romans 8:20) is a fascinating thought. His hope is that man would choose his Creator "over the pleasures of sin for a season" (see Hebrews 11:25) shows the very power of His benevolence.

Oh, don't you see it friend? Without this disposition of God's nature being a part of His attributes, He simply holds no value to us. Conversely, it would give Him no pleasure to play with man in a giant "celestial sandbox," as He is certainly not bored and in need of such entertainment. If He is arbitrary in all of His decisions, then we are but pawns and toys from within His great terrestrial toy box.

I must now speak of my personal account. I myself was a backslider for nearly ten years, which, by the way, is not a New Testament term, but we will use it for the sake of the conversation. I prefer to use the word ***reprobate*** which we aptly defined in an earlier chapter, but you see the point anyhow. I had been gloriously converted at 19 years of age and came out of an abject hedonistic lifestyle. I was also mightily baptized in the Holy Ghost and walked very tightly in righteousness with the Lord. But, after about eight years, something began to happen. Slowly, I felt the waning of God's Spirit getting further and further away from me. I began to grieve

Him with my actions and fell into a state of stale religion. I can testify first hand that the Lord was **forced** to leave, not because He **wanted** to, but simply because I didn't **need** Him anymore!

Many would say here that there is no way that God would depart since He guarantees us that "He will never leave us or forsake us." But, with a passage such as this, context is king. The apostle in this verse is referring to **provision**, not **position,** and the emphasis here is on **MATERIAL** stability, not **SPIRITUAL** stability. Let's look at the context to see the obvious point he meant to convey:

> "*Let your* conversation *be* **without covetousness;** *and be* content **with such things as ye have**: for He hath said, I will never leave thee, nor forsake thee." (Hebrews 13:5)

What is actually being conveyed here? Is it an eternal position with God that cannot be disrupted by any means of man? Or, is it a reassurance that God will not abandon us and leave us in dire material lack? Is the apostle not saying something like this: "Don't worry about needing *earthly* things, if He can so clothe the flowers, can He not take care of your needs? He's not an absentee father, He will make sure you have food and raiment. He will never be a deadbeat dad, no, not ever." I think it is obvious that Paul is here referring to our provisional status and no way implying eternal salvation.

It is erroneous, and not to mention, dangerous, to pull verses from their family and make them **orphans** apart from their "brother and sister" verses. This is where false doctrine **ALWAYS** stems from. The derelict picking of scripture, in order to fulfill a preconceived notion, has done more damage to the church than ten thousand angry sinners could ever do.

Now, back to my own account of falling away from God. I had become self-sufficient again through sin and religion, and totally lost out with Him and plunged headlong back into the world and its ways. I truly became "seven times worse" (see Matthew 12:45) in the hardness of my heart and in my pursuit of all things selfish. I had no semblance of God about me and knew without a shadow of a doubt that if I should perish, I would have split the gates of hell wide open. Therefore, not one person on this planet can convince me that you cannot lose out with God. Not only do I have the backing of the word of God, but also my own experience confirms utterly and completely that one can "lose their salvation."

The Calvinist would here argue: "See it's true, you persevered, you made it back, this proves that **perseverance** is indeed true." To that I would reply, is it not true by the word of God, that if a man turns away from God, **HE IS THE ONE** that is obligated to **come back** to his Father? Was it not true of the prodigal son? Is it not true that if an estranged soul dies in such a state, his position will be such at his death? Whether obedience unto righteousness, or sin unto death? Will his lifestyle not be frozen in time? Let's consult the prophet Ezekiel for the answer:

> "But when the righteous turneth away from his righteousness, and committeth iniquity, *and* doeth according to all the abominations that the wicked *man* doeth, shall he live? ***All his righteousness that he hath done shall not be mentioned***: in his trespass that he hath trespassed, and in his sin that he hath sinned, ***in them shall he die.*** (Ezekiel 18:24)

Now, just in case we are drawing upon the argument that this is "Old Testament stuff," let's grab a quick passage from the back of the book to reiterate our point:

> "He that is unjust, let him be ***unjust still:*** and he which is filthy, let him be ***filthy still:*** and he that is righteous, let him

be ***righteous still:*** and he that is holy, let him be ***holy still.***" (Revelation 22:11)

Clearly, The Lord here is warning that apostasy is a dangerous proposition, since one could die in his current state of disobedience and be "freeze framed" right there. Doesn't matter how a man starts, what matters to God is how he finishes. Let us look further to get even a better feel of this condition. We also must keep in mind that Israel was here accusing God of injustice for punishing those who **ONCE** walked with Him in righteousness, and had turned away. He would tell them:

"Yet saith the house of Israel, The way of the Lord is not equal. O house of Israel, are not my ways equal? are not ***your ways unequal***?" (Ezekiel 18:29)

These folks were actually engaging in a subtle form of Calvinism by accusing God of stripping them of their ***position***, simply because they were in disobedience. At last, the Lord would sum the whole matter up with His divine logic that cannot possibly be argued against in any way, shape, or form:

"Therefore I will judge you, O house of Israel, every one according to his ways, saith the Lord GOD. **REPENT**, and **TURN YOURSELVES** from all your transgressions; ***so iniquity shall not be your ruin. CAST AWAY*** from you all your transgressions, whereby ye have transgressed; and ***make you a new heart and a new spirit***: for why will ye die, O house of Israel? For I have no pleasure in the death of him that dieth, saith the Lord GOD: wherefore **TURN YOURSELVES**, and live ye." (Ezekiel 18:30-32)

Once again, it becomes obvious that the creature must do the ***repenting***, the ***turning***, and the ***casting away.*** The Lord will never interfere with such things. It is not within His nature to ***MAKE*** subjects to worship Him. Every stitch of worship in the universe, whether good or evil, is acted out with one's own volition. It cannot be otherwise and hold the essence of true worship.

There are many, many, points I would like to bring up on this subject, but it is just too exhaustive to go down those continual rabbit holes. I will just end this chapter with the following thoughts: My friend, please consider the ***why*** of the existence of the doctrine and also consider ***why you*** believe it. Search your heart and make certain there is not a hidden excuse for a pet sin. Or, maybe you are just looking for a "free, no obligation" ride into heaven. Maybe you just want a God that is noninvasive, one that simply gives you an "I.D. card" to carry in your wallet, stating that you belong to Him and that He has permanently stamped you. Maybe you just want to run your own life, build your own empire, "die with the most toys," and still be able to win out with God.

Only you know the real truth dear friend, as to whether these things reside in your heart or not. Only you know if the passion that burns in your bosom is a real tangible divine fire for the Most High, or just a flickering flame of an insurance policy that will carry you just far enough to "make it" at the end. Please, don't risk your eternity by searing your conscience with a doctrine that only pacifies the mind, yet provides no divine communion. Let us join the writer of Hebrews in his exhortation:

> "Let us draw near with a true heart in full assurance of faith, having our hearts sprinkled from an evil conscience, and our bodies washed with pure water." (Hebrews 10:22)

Chapter 17

# A WOMAN OF THE NIGHT

*"Come hither; I will shew unto thee the judgment of the great whore that sitteth upon many waters:" Revelation 17:1*

LET US BEGIN THIS CHAPTER by establishing that this entity called **Babylon** (which has taken on a plethora of interpretive attempts by the modern church), must certainly be of a nefarious nature. On that point, I think we all can agree. Over the past three decades I have heard all manner of surmisings on this subject. They include, but are not limited to, an actual city in Iraq being reconstructed as such. I have also heard many attempts to *fit* America itself into this ambiguous model. Some would even attempt to divide this entity into two Babylons, one being literal, and the other being symbolic. Many would differentiate between **Mystery Babylon,** and an actual earthly entity simply called **Babylon.**

I do not wish to bring us to the point of unnecessary jangling by drawing a distinction between the two entities. I do however want to point out a couple of things that I believe may draw us a little closer to the truth on the matter. Firstly, we must keep in mind that when the apostle uses the word "*mystery*," he is only using it to describe the convoluted *nature* of this entity's appearance and structure and not necessarily to make one Babylon distinctive from the other. John describes this woman (the harlot), as having a particular branding upon her person. Let's have a look.

> "And upon her forehead was a name written, MYSTERY, BABYLON THE GREAT, THE MOTHER OF HARLOTS AND ABOMINATIONS OF THE EARTH." (Revelation 17:5)

So, if I may paraphrase here a bit, I think we can conclude that the apostle is basically conveying the following idea: "***This Babylon is something that must be revealed by divine light,*** therefore, ***it is a MYSTERY.*** It is truth hidden from the natural eyes of reason and disclosed only to those who are open to God and privileged to know it." Based on this notion alone, we cannot simply assume that a differentiation between two Babylons (in nature), is implied here. However, we can consider that this is likely a **SPIRITUAL** kingdom that manifests in the **PHYSICAL** realm.

We do know some facts that are overtly revealed about this kingdom in this seventeenth chapter of Revelation. They are as follows:

- The woman sits upon many waters (17:1,15). (Those waters are multitudes of people all over the world affected by her rule and policies.)
- The woman rides a beast (17:1). (A kingdom, a political system, a government.)
- The woman commits fornication with kings (17:2). (She is politically active and intermingled with worldly policy.)
- The woman is dressed to the hilt in scarlet, purple, with draperies of gold and precious stones (17:4). (She is aesthetically pleasing and overly ornate in her appearance, representing

exterior religion, with no inner substance.)
- The woman is a harlot (17:5). (She is unfaithful to God and His gospel, and "cheats" with other religions. She offers her services to all who will pay her price and bow down in homage to her ways and means.)
- The woman has martyred many saints (17:6). (Many saints have been slain by "Jerusalem" and by "Rome" alike.)
- The woman is a city (17:18). (Likely Jerusalem, then transitioning to Rome and then spreading out to all the earth in the form of myriads of religions.)

With those basic premises of her attributes revealed, we can construct a consensus that may help to remove the veil that covers her true identity. Let us build our model.

This woman must be a **religious system** that has governmental powers and subsequently exercises her influence over many people from all over the world. This woman must also be a **universalist** in nature and all-inclusive (committing whoredom), embracing other religions as viable. This woman has an outward appearance of grandiose asceticism and **looks the part** of being holy and heavenly. This woman has been on a crusade to **abolish the true saints** from day one of her existence and has sought to establish her own hierarchy based on this said grandeur and false authority.

Picture this woman, if you will, as the "bride of Frankenstein" in the spiritual sense. She was brought into existence by Satan, much like that hybrid creature that Dr. Frankenstein had created in his lab when the original created monster needed a **mate**. Babylon's false fidelity was a concoction of the nuts and bolts of outward religion, assembled together with a humanistic ingenuity. This product was manufactured from the science of Satan and assembled together in order to **marry** *up* with the true church. This opposer of real bonafide gospel faith was let loose to terrorize the villages of the redeemed with her feigned and formulated religion.

This mother of menacing merchandise was designed to sell the product of outward religion through force and monetary persuasion. Her love for pomp and pristine power affords her a seat among the world's ivory towers. Her ecumenical prowess spreads even into the seats of governmental influence as she pontificates her peace-loving paradings before all the world. Her affects are so widespread that when the apostle saw her, he could only "wonder with great admiration" (see Revelation 17:6).

When Jesus arrived on the scene with the message of repentance resounding from His mouth, He would tear down the temples of temporal outward religion most ruthlessly. Following the message of John's fiery discourses on repentance, Jesus would reiterate the same message and advance it beyond the cutting down of the trees and would plant a new shoot. John would lay the ax at the root, and Jesus' death would be the seed for the new "trees of righteousness by the planting of the Lord" (see Isaiah 61:3). This new sapling would grow out of the soil of a true heart change and no longer be bound to the greenhouses of man-made religion.

When the Lord confronted the religious rectors of the day (e.g. the Scribes and Pharisees), He would scold them incessantly over their hypocrisy and outward pomp. Their lack of inward religion would draw the continual ire of the Son of God and would be the eventual demise of His own sacred, sacrificial body. The Lord would also warn His disciples constantly of the leaven of the outward religion of man, in contrast with this inward intimacy in which He was now propagating. In the gospel of Luke, He would make just such a point with these scolding statements:

> "Beware of the scribes, who like to walk around *in long robes*, and *love respectful greetings* in the market places, and *chief seats* in the synagogues and *places of honor* at banquets." (Luke 20:46)

And this famous verse:

> "Beware of false prophets, which come to you in sheep's clothing, but inwardly they are ravening wolves." (Matthew 7:15)

If we look hard enough, we can see a theme unfolding concerning our earlier constructed model of the harlot woman. The "long robes" of religion, respectful greetings, chief seats, and places of honor, would imply nothing less than a perceived *pomp* such as is expressed in regard to this woman in Revelation chapters 17 and 18. Their outward adorning of wool would conceal their inward motivation to devour households. He would also accuse them of being spiritual adulterers and committing spiritual harlotry:

> "But He answered and said unto them, an evil and *adulterous generation* seeketh after a sign; and there shall no sign be given to it, but the sign of the prophet Jonas." (Matthew 12:39)

As Jesus went on that famous tirade of rabbinical rebuke in Matthew chapter 23, we can see the indignation of a Holy God expressed through His Son. In verses 1-12 He warns His disciples, along with the rest of humanity, of this dangerous doctrinal delusion of outward religion. Let's make a quick assessment of these warnings from the Lord. Here are His indictments:

- "They say, and do not." (This is an inference to the hypocrisy of the hierarchy.)
- "They bind heavy burdens and grievous to be borne….but they themselves will not move them with one of their fingers." (These taskmasters made merchandise of their followers.)
- They "love the uppermost rooms at feasts, and the chief seats in the synagogues." (These "higher-ups" desired men's worship and admiration.)
- They love to be called "Rabbi, Rabbi." (These religious leaders wished to be highly esteemed in the eyes of all men.)

He also warns them of the following:
- "Call no **man** your father (in a religious sense), upon the earth."
- "But be not ye called Rabbi. For one is your Master, *even* Christ, and all ye are brethren." (Do not take on the personalities of the puffers and kingmakers.)
- "Neither be ye called masters." (Be sure to esteem others higher than yourselves.)
- "And whosoever shall exalt himself shall be abased, and he that shall humble himself shall be exalted." (The higher we get in the eyes of man, the lower we become in the kingdom of God.)

After His admonitions to the common folks, He turns the weapons of His words upon the merchandisers of man-made religion. His stern rebukes would shake the ecclesiastical world to its core and cause an earthquake right through the middle of the establishment. He pronounces about 8 woes on them in lightning succession and calls out their hypocrisy before all. Let us take up this lightning round of the indictments that were handed down from the courts of heaven to these criminals of criticism. In verses 13-29 He would call them:

"Proselytes, hypocrites, blind guides, false swearer's, fools, cleaners of the outward appearance while remaining full of iniquity on the inside, killers of the righteous, serpents and vipers!"

All of this, spoken to the most respected and revered religious figures of the day! Imagine the stunned crowd! Imagine the **MORE** stunned clergy! Imagine the burning in their prideful hearts to this calling out of their hidden agenda! Certainly, they would have to silence such lips of absolute truth, surely! And that, they would do by crucifying Him (at least temporarily, so they thought).

Now, let us transition back to the woman in Revelation. Notice the uncanny similarities between these rebuked zealots in Matthew 23 and her attributes? Pomp, political control, spiritual adultery, outward adornment, and the most important indictment and similarity of all, they were killers of the truly righteous! Jesus would tie it all together in one declaration with these two verses:

"Wherefore, behold, I send unto you prophets, and wise men, and scribes: and *some* of them ye shall kill and crucify; and *some* of them shall ye scourge in your synagogues, and persecute *them* from city to city." (Matthew 23:34)

And then, this telling cry over this great city's treatment of all things truly godly:

"O Jerusalem, Jerusalem, *thou* that killest the prophets, and stonest them which are sent unto thee, how often would I have gathered thy children together, even as a hen gathereth her chickens under *her* wings, and ye would not! Behold, your house is left unto you desolate." (Matthew 23:37-38)

Notice His reference to Jerusalem! "Thou that killest." Surely the Lord is in His right mind here? Surely He isn't having a conversation with a physical city? No! He is speaking to the religious **spirit** that **embodies** the city. It is the **Great Whore** of false religion! The one that God just can't convince to stay up under His wings to receive his grace! It is one that roams about freely in the storms of life, and even when the enemies rage against it, seeks to navigate its own way through them. These are those who commit spiritual adultery with the pagan ideologies and hedonisms of this world! They will simply not stay faithful in their heart no matter the extent that the Lord goes in order to express His love, even to the death of the cross!

Jesus, in the 24th chapter of Matthew would shock the religious world with these prophetic words:

> And Jesus said unto them, "See ye not all these things? Verily, I say unto you, there shall not be left here one stone upon another, that shall not be thrown down." (Matthew 24:2)

These ominous words would be fulfilled in 70 A.D. when the Roman emperor Titus decimated the city of Jerusalem. Utter destruction took place even to the degree of burning down the temple and throwing down its ornate stones while the Roman army pillaged its fine gold, as well as all its other useful artifacts. Jews would be slain by the thousands and the surviving clans would be scattered throughout the earth at that time.

Now, before we tie all of these loose strings together, let me pause here to say this. Some folks may get hung up by the fact that they believe the book of Revelation is to be interpreted in **chronological** order. They conclude that since the events in Revelation beyond chapter 3 are entirely futuristic, that Babylon simply has to be America, or an actual physical city yet to be rebuilt in Iraq. However, let us consider what the apostle John was told at the time of the vision. Was it not disclosed in the following verse very plainly, that this was a prophetic compilation of many different events, over the course of time within our dispensation of the church age?

> "Write the things which thou ***hast*** seen, and the things which ***are***, and the things which shall be ***hereafter***." (Revelation 1:19)

One must remain very open when reading this great book of Revelation. Religious prejudice and dogmatic thinking can blind us from the actual truth. Nowhere does it state in the account that it must be interpreted in a ***systematic*** order. In fact, it is clear by that previous verse, that it can either be a "***hast***," an "***are***," or a "***hereafter***." The reference here to the things "***thou hast seen***" could very well refer to the fact that John had ***already seen*** some of these things occur in his lifetime and the Lord simply led him to log them again for the future use of His church. It is also clear that the Revelation account is a collage of spiritual allegories and physical manifestations blended in such a way that the apostle, as well as ourselves, could relate to them.

Here is a case in point. Who can deny that the 12th chapter of that great book is not an historical account? The woman with the 12 crowns? (Israel). The manchild being brought forth? (The child Jesus). The dragon (Satan acting through Herod), trying to kill the baby? Can this be representative of anything but the tribes of Israel with her twelve crowns? Can this be anything other than Jesus' birth? Can the dragon be anything but Satan? You get the point. So it is very safe to say that John was seeing historic, as well as futuristic events blended together in this great spiritual tapestry.

Now in light of all that hermeneutical haggling, I believe that the destruction of Jerusalem in 70 A.D. is likely to have been the very beginning of the fulfillment of these verses in the 17th and 18th chapter of Revelation. I do also believe, however, that this "Babylon has fallen" scenario has unfolded throughout history in multi-faceted ways, and will continue to do so until the end of all things. If Babylon **BECOMES** a "habitation" **AFTER** its fall (regardless of when that has, or will yet occur), then this would no doubt have to imply a perpetuation of her effect on the world, and not a cessation of this entity's influence. In the following verse, we see that a *place to live* has been supplied by this "*fall.*" When she is brought to desolation, this simply means that **GOD Himself** no longer dwells therein. Yet, her fall has *afforded* a habitation for other entities to dwell therein and take the place of Gods departed influence

> "And he cried mightily with a strong voice, saying, "Babylon the great is fallen, is fallen, and *is become* the habitation of devils, and the hold of every foul spirit, and a cage of every unclean and hateful bird." (Revelation 18:2)

And yet another....

> "And they cast dust on their heads, and cried, weeping and wailing, saying, Alas, alas, that great city, wherein were *made rich all* that had ships in the sea by reason of her costliness! For in one hour is she *made desolate.*" (Revelation 18:19)

We must point out the word *desolate* here. This word implies that something would be made uninhabitable, or turned into a "wilderness," so to speak. If we recall from an earlier verse in Matthew 23, Jesus would tell the Jews that their "house would be left unto them ***desolate***" (Matthew 23:38). Although these are slightly different Greek words being used here in these two cases, their implications are pretty much the same. Through the rejection of the gospel message, not only would the ***physical place*** of Jerusalem be pillaged and the temple destroyed, they would also be made ***uninhabitable*** for the Lord's Spirit to dwell there. This would result in the inevitable vacating of His divine influence, leading to their "desolation."

This collapsing monolith of religious pride and pomp would crumble under the weight of the advent of the New Covenant. The old temple would come down and create this said desolation. When she ***fell*** to the ground, a ***spiritual place*** would be afforded to entities other than the Lord's Spirit. Now that Judaism was retired by God, it would be necessary for these foul birds of doctrinal bondage to have a new place to flock to. This ***Babylon*** would become a labyrinth of caverns and crevices that are now conducive for demon spirits to hide amongst. In other words, false religion would simply find new ***avenues*** and ***vehicles*** (i.e. Catholicism, denominationalism) in which to function. When God pulls Himself out of a thing, the vacuum is filled by look-alikes and mockeries after His similitude. These false religious spirits then become the replacements of ***His Spirit*** and simply take up residence within a new model.

We must also take into account the ***way*** that she has made the kings and merchants of the earth "***rich.***" This could very well imply, not just a ***material merchandise***, but a ***spiritual*** product being peddled as well. We see a little hint of this when the apostle lists all the benefits that the world has received at her hands. At the end of the list, notice the last commodity mentioned. While all else is ***material*** in nature, the last item on the list is clearly of a ***spiritual*** nature.

"And the merchants of the earth shall weep and mourn over her; for no man buyeth their merchandise any more: The merchandise of gold, and silver, and precious stones, and of pearls, and fine linen, and purple, and silk, and scarlet, and all thyine wood, and all manner vessels of ivory, and all manner vessels of most precious wood, and of brass, and iron, and marble, And cinnamon, and odours, and ointments, and frankincense, and wine, and oil, and fine flour, and wheat, and beasts, and sheep, and horses, and chariots, and slaves, and **SOULS OF MEN.**" (Revelation 18:11-13)

We may understand this part of the passage by understanding a few things. Allow us to consider the nature of whoredom (or prostitution), as we may call it in the modern vernacular. In the natural, it is actually a *trade*, or a *commerce* of a perverted nature that exchanges physical intimacy for money. Conversely, in the spiritual, it is an exchange of self-righteous works, for the benefit of a perceived spiritual intimacy.

This particular woman must inevitably be engaged in diverse degrees of spiritual fornication, since she has earned the title of the "**GREAT WHORE**" (see Revelation 17:1). But, you may ask, what is spiritual fornication? Answer: It is none other than friendship with the world! In other words, it is shaking hands with the worldly system (i.e. money, greed, lust, power, position, pomp), while yet espousing to be the "bride of Christ." The apostle James stirs our hearts to lamentation when he hits the spiritual bullseye with this arrow of truth:

"Ye adulterers and adulteresses, know ye not that the friendship of the world is enmity with God? Whosoever therefore will be a friend of the world is the enemy of God." (James 4:4)

This spiritual adultery is an indictment toward any such hypocrisy that would afford an affinity between the true Christian and the ***world***. A religion that has within it a duality of affection, is not the true religion of Jesus Christ. Rather, it is a cultivated, controllable, and man-centered perversion of the true gospel. It has no endearing faithfulness and can maneuver about freely in the Satanic system with seemingly zero angst about doing so.

Furthermore, let us consider the most important distinction being drawn here between true Christianity and this false system. A true believer who has received the Spirit of the living God will walk in true righteousness and holiness with his Lord in real bonafide intimacy. He knows His God because of that intimate union of body, soul and spirit. It is a ***spiritual marriage*** in a sense whereby we truly become one flesh with the Lord Jesus. Of course there are many obvious differences between this heavenly matrimony and the union of a physical husband and wife, but this union is of an intimate spiritual nature nonetheless. Paul spoke of this mystery in this way:

> "For we are members of His body, of His flesh, and of His bones. For this cause shall a man leave his father and mother, and shall be joined unto his wife, and they two shall be one flesh. This is a **GREAT MYSTERY**: but I speak concerning **CHRIST** and the **CHURCH**." (Ephesians 5:30-32)

So, we see here that our beloved apostle is divulging a great spiritual secret. That is the fact that God, through His Holy Spirit, can unite us with Christ in a union that is so close that we become ***one flesh with Him!*** Oh! How fabulous the mystery! How wonderful its endless boundaries! How unsearchable its riches! Union with Christ in spiritual marriage! Can it get any closer than that? I think not!

Now, let us turn back to our original point. What is the nature of prostitution? Is it not a cheap version of intimacy and a perversion of that which is reserved only for a husband and wife to engage in? Does the Bible not teach that any sexual intimacy outside of matrimony is considered fornication? So then, to **purchase** intimacy that is otherwise afforded by marriage, is not only cheap intimacy, but an insult to God-ordained matrimony.

Do you see the point unfolding here yet? Religion that is purchased by the currency of **OUR** righteousness is like a night in a cheap hotel in union with one to whom we are not espoused to. This is precisely why this Babylonian system deals in the commerce of "**THE SOULS OF MEN**," as we see in the last part of that 13th verse in chapter 18. Here me out, oh seeker! "He that hath ears let him hear!" This is of the utmost importance and no doubt the most significant point of this book! Many millions have bought, and are currently buying, her cheap version of intimacy! Her enticing perfumes, high heels, and scantily clad figure have lured many a poor soul into her licentious lare. The fragrance and charm of man-made religion is that it temporarily satisfies a burning lust within us.

- That **lust** is the self-righteousness and pride within us that needs to be recognized, acknowledged and heralded as legitimate.
- That **prostitute** is that religion that can only supply that cheap intimacy and appease that lust.
- That **payment** for intimacy is our own good works in which we offer to God as payment for our own redemption.

So let me take a breath here and summarize this whole chapter. **Babylon** is a cheap religious system that deals in the currency that proceeds from our own pockets, so to speak. She makes merchandise **of our souls** because she accepts our own works and our own abilities to get to God by the ladder of self-improvement. This is her means of commerce. We buy from her "the goods" of acceptance, flattery, and false security with the fools gold of our own goodness. She pays us the dividends with a false sense of "peace and safety" as we live under the shadows of her delusional wings. She sends us a strong delusion of a false justification, and conscience soothing salve, so that we may believe her lies (see 2 Thessalonians 2:10-11).

In that extraterrestrial telegram called the book of Revelation, Jesus would download these words to our dear apostle John in His scathing rebuke to the lukewarm Laodiceans:

> "I counsel thee to **buy of me gold** tried in the fire, that thou mayest be rich; and white raiment, that thou mayest be clothed, and *that* the shame of thy nakedness do not appear; and anoint thine eyes with eyesalve, that thou mayest see." (Revelation 3:18)

The Lord's appeal here was to the "religiously content" and the self-righteous who had "increased with goods" (see Revelation 3:17). In other words, He spoke to the ones that had sufficiency within themselves and who could not say along with Paul, "Our sufficiency is of God" (see 2 Corinthians 3:5). That "gold" that we "buy" is indeed that very infused nature of Jesus Himself that has already been tried and found faithful. It is the Spirit of His dear Son sent forth into our hearts crying "Abba Father" (see Galatians 4:6). Furthermore, that gold is only purchased by faith, received into the heart by spiritual transfusion.

In conclusion, we must consider that maybe, just maybe, we could have it all wrong. Perhaps we should not even be looking out for some futuristic, physical Babylon to manifest. Maybe we should simply be aware that her kingdom is arrayed insidiously all around us. This spiritual city needs no specific geographical home or a certain physical address, but rather, simply willing participants. This entity is willing to "fall" anywhere that affords her a "**habitation,**" a **"hold,"** or a **"cage,"** in order to work her dastardly deeds of demonic diversions upon this planet!

A religion that attempts to reach from the *inside* of man *to* the *outside* of God by its *own merits*, and one that attempts to engage in the economy of heaven with its *own currency*, is indeed the religion of Babylon. A religion that reaches from beyond the veil of the Divine, and comes ***down*** into the hearts of men, is the true religion of Jesus Christ. Oh, may we always discern the difference!

> "Every good gift and every perfect gift is from above, and cometh down from the Father of lights, with whom is no variableness, neither shadow of turning." (James 1:17)

# Chapter 18

# A MATRIARCH OF MUNICIPALITIES

*"And upon her forehead was a name written, MYSTERY, BABYLON THE GREAT, THE MOTHER OF HARLOTS AND ABOMINATIONS OF THE EARTH." Revelation 17:5*

IN 70 A.D., after the great fall of Jerusalem, Satan was then left with a bit of a dilemma. His quandary was the fact that he had lost his "seat" (or throne) of major influence he once enjoyed through a false and fettered religion. Particularly, the one that the Jews had allowed to be grossly distorted before the whole world. Satan's plethora of pagan gods have always been his attempt to cloud the judgment of mankinds seeking heart with alternative views of deity. Yet, worse than all of the false deities that he can concoct and distribute among humanity, is the perversion of the one true and living God. We see a little hint in the book of Revelation as to Satan's mode of operation in this realm of false religion. Jesus, through our dear apostle John's quill, would divulge the new location of Satan's earthly throne. He would convey the following words to the church at Pergamos:

> "I know thy works, and where thou dwellest, *even* where Satan's seat *is*: and thou holdest fast my name, and hast not denied my faith, even in those days wherein Antipas *was* my faithful martyr, who was slain among you, where Satan dwelleth." (Revelation 2:13)

As they have tried to gaze through the dimly lit veil of history, scholars have wrestled with the reason why Jesus would make this pinpointed disclosure of Satan's authoritative lair. We may ask these same questions alongside them: Why Pergamos? Why would the Lord single out this city as the pinnacle of perversion? Obviously, looking through such a glass darkly, we cannot be assured of the absolute truth on the matter. Nevertheless, we can consider something about Pergamos that may afford us a small bit of understanding on the subject. The next verse is very telling about the condition of that particular body of believers:

> "But I have a few things against thee, because thou hast there them that hold the **doctrine of Balaam,** who taught Balac to cast a stumbling block before the children of Israel, to eat things sacrificed unto idols, and to commit fornication." (Revelation 2:14)

I have neither the time, nor the space, within this book to afford me the opportunity to go into the depths of the "doctrine of Balaam." However, if you look at the account in the 22nd chapter of Numbers, you will find one central theme, and that is, **MIXTURE!** Balaam, through his own worship and sacrificial offerings unto Jehovah God, had allowed the heathen king Balac to *learn how* to worship by way of sacrifice, just like the Isrealites did. Although Balac could never entice Balaam into cursing Israel, Balaam would give him that facsimile "form of godliness" that he needed to build that model of worship in which he could coerce the children of Israel into mingling with his cultural paganism.

Now, if you look at the historical accounts of Pergamos, you will find a city that was perhaps renowned above all others of its day in regards to its paganistic paradings. She was steeped in great shrines built unto the gods of Greek culture such as Zeus, Dionysus, Athena and Asklepios. The city also sported one of the wonders of the world at that time, an altar of Zeus ascending some 40 feet in height.

Another notable attribute to this city was its use of medicinal enchantments to aid the sick. It is said that people would come and sleep in her great courtyards waiting upon the "gods" to speak to priests and physicians concerning the remedies they would need to concoct in order to heal their patients' maladies. This multitude of sorceries no doubt gave way to a plethora of euphoric religious experiences within the demonic realm.

This mecca of menacing merchandise would be called by Jesus Himself, "the seat (throne) of Satan." This center of all things corrupt would be representative of an attempt to blend those satanic false gods with the true separated gospel of Jesus Christ. From day one (at least after his failed attempt to destroy her through persecution), Satan has sought to *JOIN* the church in an unholy matrimony. The Trojan horse of learned religion has infiltrated her through the amicable means of usefulness. If Satan can join the ranks of the faithful through his mixture of the holy with the profane, alas, he has been a success.

As we fast forward some 250 years from the time of the destruction of Jerusalem, we find another interesting development unfolding in the history of the church. In the earlier chapter regarding unity, we spoke of this event called the **Council of Nicea.** We brought out the point of how the Roman emperor Constantine would attempt to blend the evangelical world together under one banner. I do not wish to engage in a history lesson or bog this book down with detailed information as all of this history can be looked into vigorously with a click of a button. The internet is full of such accounts of the history of this event and the players thereof. I want only to focus on the *essence* and *outcome* of this council as it regards a precedent that was set forth. That precedent is the word we spoke of earlier in this chapter: *MIXTURE!*

From the outside looking in, one might think this gathering of the ecclesiastical minds of the day would have inevitably produced the offspring of clarity and absolute truth. But instead, this intrusion of empirical power and governmental influence into all things sacred and separate would set an unforeseen precedent.

Let us keep in mind that the Christian experience is one of separation from the *world*. Although Israel was an *earthly* kingdom and a blend of the reign of kings and the religion of Judaism twisted together in one vine, it was but an usher and shadow of the kingdom that would soon come.

Jesus would bring a *spiritual* kingdom into being through His death, burial, and resurrection. This kingdom would no longer have the earthly tentacles that once held it in this physical realm. Before the Lord arrived on the scene, man would build that kingdom with the building blocks of self-interpretation, growing it to a place of pomp and privilege. The gospel of Jesus Christ would become a kingdom from within! One that would tear down the bricks and mortar of outward religion. He would turn to that radical, rabbinical crowd and declare:

> "Neither shall they say, Lo here! or, Lo there! For, behold, the kingdom of God is within you." (Luke 17:21)

Jesus was building a new spiritual kingdom that would be void of affiliation with earthly power and privilege. It is void of earthly governance under the priestly posterity. It is also one that was ruled separately, exclusively, and inwardly by a priesthood unseen. Oh what a plan! Cut out the middleman! Now, the Lord could have His subjects directly under the umbrella of one King, and a personal priesthood could be experienced by all!

"And from Jesus Christ, *who is* the faithful witness, *and* the first begotten of the dead, and the Prince of the kings of the earth. Unto Him that loved us, and washed us from our sins in His own blood, And hath made us kings and priests unto God and His Father; to Him *be* glory and dominion for ever and ever. Amen." (Revelation 1:5-6)

Now, let us return to this idea of Constantine and his efforts to bring those kingdoms back together again under the banner of his power and political persuasion. As an estimated 318 bishops gathered together from multiple provinces to hash out their doctrinal differences, Constantine would be the silent partner and prime mover of this man-made business of unity. Eusebius, a bishop from Caesarea who would play a dominant role in the proceedings (as far as his baptismal creed was concerned), would make this statement:

"Constantine himself proceeded through the midst of the assembly, like some heavenly messenger of God, clothed in raiment which glittered as it were with rays of light, reflecting the glowing radiance of a **PURPLE ROBE** and adorned with the brilliant splendor of **GOLD and PRECIOUS STONES**."
(source: Eusebius Pamphilius, The Life of Constantine [Vita Constantini] Book 3, chapter 10).

Now, let us consider this uncanny resemblance between the woman in Revelation, and this gayla affair conducted by the Emperor:

"The woman was dressed in **PURPLE** and scarlet, and adorned with **GOLD** and **PRECIOUS STONES** and pearls. She held in her hand a golden cup full of abominations and the impurities of her sexual immorality." (Revelation 17:4)

These striking similarities should indeed draw up an eyebrow on even the most staunchest of skeptics. The abominations in that golden cup is the **MIXTURE** of the world's political powers with God's heavenly religion in Christ Jesus. The "impurities of her sexual immoralities" are no doubt that "fornication with the kings of the earth (see Revelation 17:2), and consequently, not the true religion of Jesus Christ. That cocktail of contrived consecration is the intoxicant of man-made religion being slipped insidiously back into the punch bowl of the sacred wine of the kingdom.

Hence! Babylon had found her new home and could comfortably fall back into her place among the kingdoms of this world in a perfect blend of religion and state. She has been growing exponentially ever since, overshadowing nearly every facet of Christianity in one form or another. Although she would not *officially* blend wholly church and state until about 380 A.D. with the ***Edict of Thessalonica,*** her blueprint of organized religion would be drafted in that drawing room of the religious architects of Constantine's day. It would become the navigational tool that would start in the Catholic (universal) institution of organized religion and permeate throughout the ages, thus affecting the entire lump with her leaven of compromise and mixture with the world.

Let us pause right here for a moment to say something extremely significant. No one should doubt, based on the historical accounts readily found in the archives of the Catholic Church, as well as history in general, the maniacal abuse she has dealt to her perceived heretical dissidents. Some have estimated (on average), 40,000 martyrs a year have died at her hands (source John Dowling, The History of Romanism, pp. 541-542). Her judgment is no doubt stored in the cup of God's wrath. Yes, she is drunk on the blood of the saints, as were the perpetrators of martyrdom that Jesus rebuked in the Jewish state when He was on the earth.

In light of all that terrible history of the Catholic Church and her obvious correlation to this great whore in Revelation, I want to proceed beyond this fulfillment of prophecy and look at something even more insidious. Most would stop here well short of the main gist of this whole scheme of Satan and would be satisfied to say something like this: "Yes, with that old Catholic Church and her pomp and power and ecumenical blendings with the world's religions and her martyring of the saints, I can sure see how she could be Babylon." But, let us not forget the subtlety of the serpent. While he is performing an obvious magic trick before our eyes, he is reaching inconspicuously around us to steal our wallets from our back pocket. In other words, he never plateaus on deception, he always takes it higher on up his menacing mountain of lies.

So, here we must stop and remind ourselves that this woman called Babylon cannot necessarily be traced to any **ONE** religious sector. She is a ***spiritual*** kingdom, remember, and she is always looking for a new place to ***fall*** in the material world. She simply finds her home in the comforts of any form of organized religion.

The closer one gets to absolute truth, the greater the counteraction of deception will be. Chess games start off very quickly, but as the pieces disappear, the game slows to a deliberate and more thoughtful pace. Such it is with the pure gospel in its full power. Satans need to focus and to concentrate becomes much more astute when the true church begins to stand erect. He must constantly try and stay ahead of the game if he is to quell and stymie the forward momentum of Zion. Therefore, he must create a pre-formed, functional, and chiseled-out religion to facilitate any perceived outbreaks of true movement in the divine realm. If he can turn a ***movement*** into a ***monument***, he has won that part of the battle. Institutionalized religion awaits with open arms to any seeker of absolute truth along his path to fullness. Oh, but press on dear one! For

"Surely He shall deliver thee from the snare of the fowler, *and* from the noisome pestilence" (Psalm 91:3).

With that said, let us take note that this parading prostitute of aestheticism is in fact a **MOTHER!** She has mouths to feed! Many millions are "heaping to themselves" plates of palatable dainties from the tables of her deception. She has offspring in nearly every church basement. She is multiplying like mice in her exponential take-over of the neglected and dark areas of the church's unlit underbelly.

Denominationalism, in its sectarian and segregational posture, has indeed been born out of this same ideology. This **mother of merchandise** goes all the way back to Jerusalem with her diabolical schemes of trapping men and chaining them to her "dog-ma house." It simply does not matter whether it be Judaism, Catholicism or Protestantism, as long as the *concept* is of the same model. These babies that were born out of her womb at the time of the Reformation may indeed *seem* a bit different in appearance and scope, but the genes that flow through their bloodstream are of the same DNA. Many men "*came out of her*" at that time. However, she did not come completely ***out of them***. Instead, they brought a little piece of that mother with them and began the procreation of the hybrid model of the mixture of God and man-made religion.

I call this the "exclusivity complex." It is the same incubator that produces the offspring of its own religious kind, whether it be the Papacy or the Protestant pulpit. When man deviates from the flow of the divine essence of his religion, he gets up off his knees of humility and pulls his chair up to his desk of higher learning. It is then and there that he breaks his connective umbilical cord to the kingdom. It is here that the children of reason are born and the orphans of spiritual power are abandoned. Structure is born out of the *absence* of the dynamic

***transformative power*** of the Spirit, and becomes a "hold, a cage, and a habitation" for the next generation of foul birds.

Many movements have started in the Spirit and ended in the flesh. Paul's admonition to the Galatians could very well apply here: "Ye did run well; who did hinder you that ye should not obey the truth?" (Galatians 5:7). It would, at this point, do us no good to name the plethora of denominational beginnings that have had their foundation in "repentance from dead works, and faith towards God" (see Hebrews 6:1). However, let us just say that it's not how you start that matters, but how you finish that takes the prize. "Do you not know that those who run in a race all run, but one receives the prize? Run in such a way that you may obtain *it*." (1 Corinthians 9:24).

As these generational giants called ***denominations*** became more and more tainted with human reasoning, they would forsake the inflow of the Spirit and take on the voting powers of carnal men. They would once again reflect the image of that very mother that they sought to leave behind, the very one they had left originally, in order to cleave unto Christ alone.

Some may argue that Christianity ***should*** be an organized religion and consequently be equipped with the hierarchies and overseers of canonical control. To that I would say, indeed she is to be conducted "decently and in order" (see 1 Corinthians 14:40), but this can only be achieved through the word of God and prayer. We simply cannot employ reasoning and ecumenical musings to something so sacred as the ways of God. This affords the Devil a foothold that he needs in order to come through the cracked open door with his institutional interference and systematic sublimities.

In Acts 15, the apostles did indeed have a meeting at Jerusalem to work out the questionable issues raised at Antioch concerning the need for the Gentiles to be circumcised. We can also be fairly certain that much discussion was engaged in before they arrived at their consensus. So let us ask, what is the difference between such a meeting in the first church, and this council in the 4th century conducted under Constantine? A meeting that was ***also*** perceived as an attempt to bring about unity? The clear difference is the ***MEANS*** employed in the two events. The first church did not call upon any form of human government, man-made authority, or input from the world, to make those judgment calls. In other words, there was no ***MIXTURE.***

The whole scene in the 4th century was wrong from the start. Constantines use of the earthly throne as an influence would afford a latent blending of pagan culture with the resurrection of Jesus, thereby creating the hybrid known as "Easter" (which was never instituted by the early church). Many would debate that this first Easter was ***not*** blended with paganism and that it was not originally the cultural mixture that has since morphed into. Regardless of whether this can be proven or not, the ***model*** that was created would afford an incubator for such hybrid mixtures to germinate over time. Yet, even more importantly than this, is this subtle attempt to bring back ***customs*** into the church. This opening of the door to ***traditions*** would be eerily reminiscent of Judaism's attempt to infiltrate the church at Galatia. This ***Council of Nicea*** was no doubt the reawakening of that same religious spirit that Paul contended with in that body of believers.

Paul would express this lament over the Galatians breaking off from the simplicity that is in Christ and their returning to the old school of religious observation. We have to wonder, would he have rebuked this gathering of the religious minds of the day under Constantine's watch with the same admonition?

> "But now, after that ye have known God, or rather are known of God, how turn ye again to the weak and beggarly elements, whereunto ye desire again to be in bondage? Ye observe **days**, and **months**, and **times**, and **years**. I am afraid of you, lest I have bestowed upon you labor in vain." (Galatians 4:9-11)

Obviously it didn't stop there. As Constantine marched on in his endeavors, he would establish the precedent of setting by-laws and boundaries for clerical hierarchy to fit nicely in place among the thrones of men. The voting system and **confirmation** of men of God would be placed into the hands of back rooms and boardrooms of religious hierarchy. That divine ordination would no longer be seen as something that flowed down from God, as was Paul's celestial commision. Our apostle would pen these words in his intro to the Galatians (that every man of God should live by), to those same folks who would stumble back into formalism:

> "Paul, an apostle, **not of men, neither by man**, but by Jesus Christ, and God the Father, who raised Him from the dead." (Galatians 1:1)

Oh, this is the trap of all traps! To be lured back to the redlight district of organized religion! To answer the calls of her perverted intimacy is to embrace a cold, dead, loveless and lifeless entanglement with ritualism. Oh, may we return to a time of God-called men! Men that have been sprinkled with the heavenly mist of power, saturated with the oil of the anointing, and ordained through declaration of the very mouth of God! Let us flee from the whorehouse of confined religion and escape her wrath that slumbereth not! For in one hour, her desolation cometh! May we not be caught under the sheets with this woman of the night!

This woman, whether sitting in the chief seats in the temple in Jerusalem, or the great Papal throne in the Vatican, or even in the boardrooms of denominational bureaucracy, has but one central theme. She is religion not born of spiritual spontaneity, but one that is contrived out of a formality of dull dogmatism. Let us repent of our fornication with her and return to the holy matrimony of a glorious bride, free of Babylon's spots and wrinkles!

> "For I am jealous over you with godly jealousy: for I have espoused you to one husband, that I may present you as a chaste virgin to Christ." (2 Corinthians 11:2)

Chapter 19

# BATS IN THE BELL TOWER

*"And he cried mightily with a strong voice saying Babylon the great is fallen, is fallen, and is become the habitation of devils and the hold of every foul spirit and a cage for every unclean and hateful bird." Revelation 18:2*

IN THE PREVIOUS COUPLE OF CHAPTERS, we took a glimpse at the nature of this entity called Babylon. We were able to draw some similarities between the different dispensations of her multifaceted manifestations down through time. Let us now take the time to examine the *means* by which she carries out her doctrinal diversions. We have also uncovered a handful of the offspring of her many misconstrued and misleading teachings throughout this book. However, we must now descend deeper into her conniving caves and see how this personally affects you and I, whether we be leaders or laity.

These entities spoken of in this 2nd verse in Revelation 18 (devils, foul spirits, and unclean birds), must no doubt be referring to those spirits that are sent out to deceive and to divert mankind from all things truthful. These are the carriers of doctrinal poison sent out to infect the unsuspecting body of Christ. The primary mission of these menacing creatures of the air is to rob the church of its purity and power. The reference here to things that are capable of flight would imply their mission and scope is one of a *courier* position. Interesting here also, is the reference to a "caged bird," which would be indicative of the imprisonment and confinement of man-made religion with its rites and rituals.

This Babylonian religious system that they proceed from is composed of various and sundry elements of a *mixture* of truth and lies. These confusing teachings are the confounded languages of many diverse spiritual entities. The very meaning of the word **Babylon** means: "gate of god(s)"(- source: Bible Hub/Strong's word #897) and is indicative of her agenda. This gate to the second heavens, where principalities and powers rule over the darkness, is the entry point of all things religiously nefarious in the universe. This religious principle of constructing for ourselves great towers of notability, in order to be recognised as viable creatures, goes all the way back to the building of a tower in Genesis 11. This "tower of Babel," which was constructed by the general consent of all of mankind, represents the endeavor of we humans to reach God by our *own means*. This is, in essence, the nature of all religious exercises that are outside of the pure gospel of Jesus Christ. Consider this account of the incident in verse 4:

> "And they said, Go to, let us build us a city and a tower, whose top *may reach* unto heaven; and **let us make us a name**, lest we be scattered abroad upon the face of the whole earth." (Genesis 11:4)

Oh, it is right here my friend, plainly seen before all of the universe! Man, by influence of the "god of this world" (Satan), has within him this same reflection of the one formerly called **Lucifer**. It is nothing less than the very disposition of the Devil himself, found within our very own hearts. This is what causes man to rise up and build great ascendancies into the clouds of personal endeavor. We see it clearly here in Isaiah, how this disposition plays out on the world's stage:

"How art thou fallen from heaven, O Lucifer, son of the morning! *How* art thou cut down to the ground, which didst weaken the nations! For thou hast said in thine heart, ***I will*** ascend into heaven, ***I will*** exalt my throne above the stars of God: ***I will*** sit also upon the mount of the congregation, in the sides of the north: ***I will ascend above the heights of the clouds; I will be like*** the Most High. Yet thou shalt be brought down to hell, to the sides of the pit." (Isaiah 14:12-15)

Ever since that fall of man in the garden, Satan and his cohorts have been on a mission. That mission is to bring about a revolt within the heart of man, not unlike his very own documented anarchy within the biblical account. The serpent and his beguiling methods are as slippery as his very own underbelly. If he can convince man that he has within himself some element of good, and a capacity to carry out a righteous pursuit of communion with the Divine, he has them within his striking distance.

This is the essence of man-centered religion, and the insidious nature of the ***antichrist*** spirit that pervades through the entirety of the planet. An "anti" Christ spirit is not necessarily a spirit that is in the state of overt blatant rebellion against God, but instead, is a ***substitute*** for Christ dwelling within us. Indeed, the end result is rebellion, but the prime mover is "to be like God" in a state of self-righteousness, all the while trying to please God in the flesh. The definition in the Greek will afford us a better view of this word ***antichrist***:

> "properly, opposite to Christ; someone acting ***in place of*** (*against*) Christ;" (source: Bible Hub/ Strong's word #500)

We can also see by this definition, as it is used in the book of 1 John, that it implies a **SPIRIT** that is a **REPLACEMENT** for Christ. This is why the apostle would say:

"Little children, it is the last time: and as ye have heard *that antichrist* shall come, even now are there *many antichrists*; whereby we know that it is the last time." (1 John 2:18)

If I could indulge in a paraphrase here, I think we would find the apostle saying something like this: "Beloved, beyond the fact that you expect a man to emerge, that would proclaim himself to be the Messiah, look around you and you will find the air charged with a spirit. 'The prince of the power of the air' has permeated the very atmosphere with a spirit of professional religion. It is a religion that substitutes the indwelling Christ, with the mimicry of the manifested works of the flesh. It has not the spontaneity of the Spirit, but has instead its origin in a look-a-like servitude."

This was Satan's appeal in the garden of Eden and this appeal has never changed in its dynamics over the centuries. In fact, this lie has only evolved in its methods of delivery, while the central lie has remained the same. The appetizing appeal of that lie is none other than this, "You will be like God, knowing good and evil" (see Genesis 3:5). This antichrist anthem rings out from the clamoring gongs of religion, and emits from the tinkling bells of the Babylonian model of self-worth.

These doctrines of devils have their appeal in the five senses of achievement and within the central nervous system of our very own pride. We are not unlike "our father the devil" (see John 8:44), in our endeavors of self-will and self-dependency. It's only through experiencing the humility of this true Christ that we are able to cry, "Oh wretched man that I am" (see Romans 7:24). There is only one way that we can experience the remedy for the serpent in our bosom, and that is by receiving this indwelling Christ.

When considering the nature of these false doctrines, one must consider a few things that afford them their place among humanity.

Namely, their dwelling places, their legal rights of citizenship, and their intentions of dwelling there.

Firstly, we must ask, what is the nature of this dwelling place? As we had spoken of in previous chapters, her *fall* is one that *facilitates* something, rather than utterly **destroying** her. Notice again in the scripture reference this allusion to a "habitation, a hold, and a cage." This implies that a place has been afforded somehow and that an accommodation has been supplied for these unclean, foul, and demonic birds. Since this is obviously figurative language and not dealing with specific geographics, it would have to imply that this dwelling place must certainly refer to a ***state of things***, rather than a physical limitation of some kind.

Attractive conditions must exist to afford them such accommodations. This would make it possible for these doctrinal birds to have a place to live, and, consequently, have a place to survive this side of the abyss. In the 2nd epistle of Paul the apostle to Timothy, he speaks of a condition most alarming in the church. It is the condition of "easy believism." This pampering pretense of piety is a sickness of seduction, a contagion of complacency, and a pandemic of pridefulness. Many today are simply trying to load up their plate with an easier, more palatable portion of digestible truths that go easily down the throat!

> "For the time will come when they will not endure sound doctrine; but after their own lusts shall they heap to themselves teachers, having itching ears." (2 Timothy 4:3)

In this prophecy, we see an unwillingness to **endure** the truth of the Gospel and a giving way to a more efficient streamline approach. Their modern fast-paced lifestyles would clamor for a more convenient version of religion that could fit within the calendars of their preconceived ambitious agendas. The inevitable result is an approach that does not require the giving up of the self life, instead, it takes a light view of sin and thereby affording a license for iniquity. As we can clearly see, the origin of this **"heaping"** finds itself in the phrase, ***"After their own lust."*** This statement implies that the very existence of such loose teachings have their foundation in the base passions of man.

These doctrinal devils are ever ready to offer a more fleshly appeal to any soul who deviates from the pure and enduring message of the gospel. If an individual desires a certain **brand** of gospel and a tailored doctrinal suit of his or her own liking, they can readily find it. One only needs to go window shopping for their own fitted version of the gospel and it will not take long before you find yourself, with money in hand, gazing through the window of a local religious institution. You will soon find that they are buying and selling the gospel on nearly every block of your city in one form or another.

This blends directly into my next point in question. What are the legal rights of these dirty doctrinal birds? In other words, why are they allowed to have such sway among the church? It seems that navigating through the modern plethora of teachings is like driving through a blizzard with no windshield wipers, which makes it very hard to see.

It almost seems unfair at times, the conditions we have found ourselves in and the difficulty in navigating our way through to the truth of the real gospel. Why so many opinions? Why so many interpretations? Why so many denominations? All of these questions fly around in our heads as we seek to find our way in this dark time. You may ask, "So, why is it that such clouds have been allowed to descend upon the house of God? Why the fog of misleading and reckless doctrinal haze?" I think the answer is clear if we look hard enough. It is quite simply that there is a demand for it! Notice this verse by Paul in the second epistle to the Thessalonians:

"And for **this cause** God shall send them strong delusion, that they should **believe a lie:** That they all might be damned who believed not the truth, but **had pleasure in unrighteousness.**"
(2 Thessalonians 2:11-12)

So, we can see that there is an obvious reason why a strong delusion is sent forth by God. It is quite simply because of the lack of adherence to truth and the pleasure in unrighteousness. This is what brings the bats to the bell tower! Consider what it is that attracts a bat (doctrinal devils). Is it not the density of darkness? These creatures of the night love darkness and they need a place away from the light to accommodate their feastings, as well their nestings. What better place than a church bell tower? What a more convenient locale! Hiding in plain sight, high above all humans, unsuspectedly living right in the upper chambers of the synagogue! No one notices, no one is alarmed, not even a bell ringing on Sunday morning can scare them out into the light! No, they do all their work in the cover of darkness when the souls of men are asleep! This is when they do their feasting.

We must then conclude that these menacing mammals of night flight, called false doctrines, have their right of occupancy granted by the **church itself.** Herein lies their legal rights: "pleasure in unrighteousness." This is what brings forth a strong delusion and, consequently, brings forth false doctrine. Demand, demand, demand!!

The third and final consideration we must take into account is: What is the intent of these foul birds? It would seem obvious that a malicious motive is indeed the prime mover, but what is the **means** and the **end** of it? This would imply that there would have to be willing couriers of such doctrines. Therefore, it is safe to assume that the **ministry** would be the most sought after target for their pernicious perchings. These foul birds seek to light upon the shoulders of the pontificators of the pulpit. This is the highest profile place for them to land, thereby affording them the most effective vantage point. Here, they can cover more ground by deceiving the man with the mic. Hence, they influence more souls, more quickly. They must convince the clergy of their schemes in order to break the breach, since he is the gatekeeper of truth.

A man out of touch with God, is a man in touch with devils! This can only stand to reason: "He that is not with me is against me, and he that gathereth not, scatters abroad" (see Matthew 12:30). If a man has an audience in any format, or a platform within the parameters of organized religion, he is a target for all such foul birds! "Get me the leader's ear!" is the cry of the Devil! This is the surefire way for Satan to break down a system. It is to find its strongest citadel, and then begin the systematic removal of its foundational bricks, so that its tower will come down. Oh, beware, man of God! You are the channel of truth, or the channel of error, depending on the state of your own heart and its propensity to truth, or its attraction to compromise. Paul states it so fittingly in his letter to Timothy:

> "But evil men and seducers shall wax worse and worse, deceiving and being deceived." (2 Timothy 3:13)

We see by this passage that deception self-perpetuates. It is a dynamo that continues to move in a direction that culminates to the end of all things. Oh, how many times did the apostle see this in the prophetic scope! Looking afar off, he saw our time, ripe with the fruits of seductions and seditions. Like wax running over a candle and hardening as it gets too far from the flame, so are the cold hearts of humanity as they push further away from the fires of truth. Here in the cold distance from the flames of passion, they find themselves on the perimeter of error.

The intentions of these "birds" are very clear. It is to remove the head (Jesus), away from the body (the church). Consequently, they have successfully drawn it away from the center focus of a simple relationship with Christ. If these foul birds can divert souls away from the flame of passion for the heart of God, then they have achieved their goal. "Anything but Christ himself!" is their cry. "Let us lay down the breadcrumbs of diversion and teach them something **about** Christ, and they will pursue another lover and leave off their pursuit of Christ **alone**." Their anthem thus rings. "Detach them from the head and the body will die." This is a very plain and simple technique, but very effective indeed. Paul would warn of such a dilemma occurring to the Colossian believers:

> "And not holding to the Head from which all the body by joints and bands having nourishment ministered and knit together increases with the increase of God." (Colossians 2:19)

As we wrap up this chapter, let us ask ourselves this major question: What is our protocol henceforth? How can we be truly reattached to the head? I would simply answer those questions with a couple of others…. Are we indeed willing to step back, apply the eye salve, and take this spiritual spanking we have coming to us? Are we willing to do **whatever** it takes to stem the tide of falseness that has flooded Zion?

I think the prophet Joel would take us to that answer more quickly than any other that I can readily think of. Let's allow him to take us to the end of this particular thought:

"Therefore also now, saith the LORD, turn ye *even* to me with all your heart, and with fasting, and with weeping, and with mourning:

And rend your heart, and not your garments, and turn unto the

LORD your God: for He *is* gracious and merciful, slow to anger, and of great kindness, and repenteth Him of the evil.

Who knoweth *if* He will return and repent, and leave a blessing behind Him; *even* a meat offering and a drink offering unto the LORD your God?

Blow the trumpet in Zion, sanctify a fast, call a solemn assembly:

Gather the people, sanctify the congregation, assemble the elders, gather the children, and those that suck the breasts: Let the bridegroom go forth of His chamber, and the bride out of her closet.

Let the priests, the ministers of the LORD, weep between the porch and the altar, and let them say, Spare thy people, O LORD, and give not thine heritage to reproach, that the heathen should rule over them: Wherefore should they say among the people, Where *is* their God?

Then will the LORD be jealous for His land, and pity His people.

Yea, the LORD will answer and say unto His people, Behold, I will send you corn, and wine, and oil, and ye shall be satisfied therewith: and I will no more make you a reproach among the heathen:

I will remove far off from you the northern *army*, and will drive him into a land barren and desolate, with his face toward the east sea, and his hinder part toward the utmost sea, and his stink shall come up, and his ill savor shall come up, because he hath done great things.

Fear not, O land; be glad and rejoice: for the LORD will do great things." (Joel 2:12-21)

> Oh, do hear it men and women of God! It is our only hope in these troubled times of preposterous apostasy! Let God break our hearts over these overtly degenerate spiritual conditions! May God help us!

## Chapter 20

# A SNUFFED OUT CANDLE

*"Remember therefore from whence thou art fallen, and repent, and the first works; or else I will come unto thee quickly, and will remove thy candlestick out of his place, except thou repent." Revelation 2:5*

IF YOU WERE TO ASK THE MAJORITY of the modern clergy if they desired God to *move* in their church body, they would no doubt answer with a resounding: "Yes, of course, this is the reason we *do* church." If you were to turn that question on the overall population of the pew, you would no doubt be met with the same answer. Although there are pockets of complacency throughout all assemblies known as the "chosen frozen" (as the old hardline Pentecostals used to call them), the majority of folks attend church for at least *some* advancement of their idea of God.

When the Son of God came back around 90 A.D. to translate that beloved apostle John into the 3rd heavens in order to receive that grand vision of the Revelation, He would make an earthly visit to him first. He would appear to him in great glory and John would testify that "His eyes *were* as a flame of fire" (see Revelation 1:14). These flames were no doubt a reflection of His passion for His church. This visit would prostrate John to the ground and reiterate that same zeal that is within the nature of Christ that caused Him to clear the tables of the merchandisers in His Fathers temple. Yes, this same bosom that John had laid his head on some 60 years prior, now resounded "with the voice of many waters" (vs. 15).

As the Lord made His rounds to the various churches in His attempt to straighten out their crooked places, He would start His great uncovering at Ephesus. Let me just pause here to make an important observation. Many in the church today would say that these 7 churches represent 7 **sections** of the history of the church over the past 2000 years. Many would also say that we are in the Laodicean age of this dispensation and thereby making it the last segment of the church age. Although I would concur that we in the modern church are indeed "increased with goods and have need of nothing" and in a "lukewarm" condition, I think it may be a bit disingenuous to assume that the Lord was here trying to unveil a systematic **time-released** pattern.

I think it is very safe to say that these churches were very **real** assemblies and therefore can be used universally as an example all throughout the church age. We cannot discount any of them under the assumption that much of it is past, and impertinent, any more than we can say so of the Old Testament. I think we can safely say with Paul that the following principle can apply here as well.

> "Now all these things happened unto them for ensamples: and they are written for our admonition, upon whom the ends of the world are come." (1 Corinthians 10:11)

Now, with that established, let's go back to our beginning verse concerning the removal of the "candlestick." We can clearly understand by the following text that these candlesticks represent the actual assemblies.

## A SNUFFED OUT CANDLE

"The seven candlesticks which thou sawest are the seven churches." (Revelation 1:20)

However, beyond the fact of their representative inference to the churches, they certainly must also represent something that can be "removed" (see Revelation 2:5). Jesus here warns the Ephesians of something very subtle that has taken place in their assembly. That was, in the course of "doing church," they had overlooked the essential nature of their Christian experience.

In the second verse, He would disclose the fact that His all-seeing eyes had scanned the assembly thoroughly enough to see a distinction hidden beneath all of their "churchianity." Let us look closely at this 2nd verse:

"I know **thy** works, and **thy** labor, and **thy** patience." (Revelation 2:2)

To most, this would seem as a noble commendation to a busy church who had even "tried them which say they are apostles, and are not, and hast found them liars" (vs. 2). However, when we see the same commendation repeated in the 3rd verse, it has with it a different accompanying word:

"And **hast** borne, and **hast** patience, and for my name's sake **hast** labored, and **hast** not fainted." (Revelation 2:3)

Notice here that the previous usage of "thy" had now been substituted for "hast." One may ask, why the change up? Is it even important? Does it affect the dynamics? Indeed it does, and that exceedingly. Here, the Lord was distinguishing, not between the **works** themselves, but the prime mover **behind** them. I believe He was trying to convey something like this:

> "I know **THY** works! That which proceeds out of **YOURSELF!** But I also know that there was a time when you **HAST** (been in possession of) something of **MINE!**"

Oh, do we see the misstep here!? These folks had carried on in the same works as they had always performed, but had lost the essential ingredient. In verse 4, the Lord indicts them with this humbling admonition, "Thou hast left thy first love." He would also issue this piercing rebuke to "Remember therefore from whence thou art *fallen,* and repent, and do the first works" (vs. 5). I find it more than ironic that we have just navigated through the chapters of the mighty Babylon that had *fallen,* and we find ourselves right in the middle of the same sort of language concerning this church in Ephesus, "Thou art *fallen.*"

Paul the apostle speaks of this same "*falling away*" (apostasy) in that 2nd of his epistles to the Thessalonians. He would also tell the Galatians that "Whosoever of you are justified by the law; ye are *fallen* from grace" (Galatians 5:4).

In the kingdom of God, to go **higher**, is actually the state of *falling.* Whenever the endeavors of men, regardless of the plethora of virtuous acts he may ascribe to his account, spring from anything except pure divine love, it brings spiritual death. This upside down kingdom works from the bottom up. In other words, the more dependent you are, the more grace you will receive. The majority of the modern church, much like the Ephesians, have left that *intimacy* with God and the dependency thereof, and have opted rather to love their own **works.**

To "fall from grace," is simply to lose the divine flow in a thing. When man loses that position of a "conduit" for the grace of God, his pipes become clogged with reason, intuition, and engineering. When the Spirit ceases to flow in His life-giving *fountain*, He is sadly replaced with a "cistern that can hold no water" (see Jeremiah 2:13). Works then turn into philanthropic appeasement of the conscience rather than the mentality that can say "We are unprofitable servants: we have done that which was our duty to do" (see Luke 17:10).

So, let us go back to the subject of the **candlestick.** What is it? How is it removed? To help answer these questions, I will need to relay a vision that I experienced some time ago while in prayer. In this vision, I saw a very dark room with many folks crawling on the floor. Although it was almost pitch black, I was somehow able to see the people groping the wall with their hands. While on their knees, they were searching diligently on the wall around the height of the top of their heads. It seemed to be a scene of alarm, as if these victims desperately needed light to rescue themselves from this dark room. The interpretation to this vision, which lasted less than a minute, came quickly after it ended. Again, this is a paraphrase of what I was told, as it was several years ago: "I am going to remove my candlestick from the modern church so that they once again grope for the light switch. They have too long been satisfied in their waning light, I must therefore remove my influence from their assemblies so that they will know to seek for me once again." This scene, and the description thereof, made very real this verse in Isaiah:

> "We grope for the wall like the blind, and we grope as if we had no eyes: we stumble at noonday as in the night; we are in desolate places as dead men." (Isaiah 59:10)

Ah, there it was! It wasn't that Jesus was telling the Ephesians that He was going to ***remove their church*** from existence altogether, but rather, that He was going to ***remove Himself from their church***, and thereby remove His ***influence within*** the assembly! Yes, the church would indeed go on, but she would be just like a "cicada shell" hanging on a tree. Even after its life was gone from it, it would remain intact, but only as a facsimile of the real essence that it once possessed.

When the apostle Paul wrote his letter to the Ephesians some 30 years prior to that celestial telegram from John, he would pray an imperative prayer for them. As Paul knelt before God, he would express his earnest prayer of desire for them to stay the course in pursuit of the higher place in God. Oh what a prayer it was! We should always echo this prayer for the church, as it is the ultimate will of God for His people!

> "Wherefore I also, after I heard of your faith in the Lord Jesus, and love unto all the saints, Cease not to give thanks for you, making mention of you in my prayers; That the God of our Lord Jesus Christ, the Father of glory, may give unto you the Spirit of wisdom and revelation in the knowledge of Him: The eyes of your understanding being enlightened; that ye may know what is the hope of His calling, and what the riches of the glory of His inheritance in the saints, And what *is* the exceeding greatness of His power to us-ward who believe, according to the working of His mighty power, which He wrought in Christ, when He raised Him from the dead, and set *Him* at His own right hand in the heavenly *places*." (Ephesians 1:15-20)

This prayer truly needs no explanation, it is the essence of the hope of the Holy Spirit for the Christian experience. That hope is that each person, that has come to an actual faith in Jesus and has been transformed by His power, would keep moving onward and upward into the heights of God. Paul was expressing nothing less than the will of God for us to experience the Lord's fullness! The "hope of His calling," is nothing less than that fullest expression of His power and virtue within our heart that we can possibly contain. These are the "riches of the glory" that "the eyes of our understanding" must be "enlightened" to.

Oh, how shortchanged is the modern church of this! How far below the waterline her vessel sails! Weighted down with the cargo of this life and its anxieties! Dashed to pieces on the coral reefs of compromise and complacency! May God's Spirit help the old ship of Zion to lighten her load and once again float high upon the waves, far above the risk of being swamped by the world's flooding tempests.

Men and women of God, it is time for a long overdue inventory of your assembly. Let us **honestly** ask ourselves these questions. Have the lights gone out? Is the candle gone? Is the divine influence truly there? Is the conviction of God's Spirit in your midst? Is righteousness the keynote speaker in your pulpit, or has the mic been yielded to a subtle seducer of excuses for iniquity? Oh friends, there isn't much time until "the darkness shall cover the earth, and gross darkness the people" (Isaiah 60:2).

We have somehow allowed *our* callings to *work* for Him in ministry, to supersede *His* calling for us to *know* Him! We work tirelessly at the grinding mills of organized religion, while He seeks just as earnestly to "work **IN** us, both to will and to do of His good pleasure" (see Philippians 2:13). We work incessantly to reveal His Son *to the world*, while He, in His ardent passion, attempts to reveal His Son *in us.*

We end this chapter with a promise and declaration from the apostle Peter as to what God has actually called us to. We also must end with the Lord's admonition to once again, "make straight paths" in the assembly for the Son of God to walk amongst His candlesticks!

"According as His divine power hath given unto us all things that *pertain* unto life and godliness, through the knowledge of Him that hath **called us** to **glory and virtue.**" (2 Peter 1:3)

"Remember therefore from whence thou art fallen, and repent, and **do the first works**; or else I will come unto thee quickly, and will remove thy candlestick out of his place, except thou repent." (Revelation 2:5)

Our "first works" is to burn with the passion of knowing Him, the passion of loving Him, and the passion of experiencing Him. May we get back to the low places, that we might ascend into the high and lofty place with Him! Amen.

## Chapter 21

# A NOMAD KING

*And Jesus said to him, "The foxes have holes, and the birds of the air nests; but the Son of Man has nowhere He might lay His head." Luke 9:58*

WE STARTED THIS BOOK with a question that we attempted to answer throughout its pages.

That question was: What do you want from God?

As we draw near to its conclusion, it is only fitting that we end it with one as well.

That question is: What does God want from you?

If you have made it as far as this chapter, perhaps this question takes on a different meaning than before you entered the pages of this book. Maybe now you can be honest, maybe now you can answer: "I am not sure." Or, maybe you knew all along and this chapter has no relevance to you. Whatever the case, this is a question that **MUST** be answered by every free-will creature.

In this day and age of introverted gospels and self-help superstars, we have lost something very endearing. That is the fact that we have somehow missed the very essence of *why* the good news is in fact *good* news! When we listen to the majority of the modern pulpits pontificate their doctrines, we find a disturbing theme woven throughout their discourses.

There is an appeal proceeding forth from these once sacred podiums that has within it a backwards theology of sorts. It is gospel that is indeed **good news**, but it is good news that is offered to the **wrong side** of man.

When the Lord Jesus arrived on the scene, He would make straight the path of the many crooked ideologies about His Father in which the clergy had erroneously propagated. Mankind, through the perversions of Satan, had found themselves as a whole, out of touch with a living God. The cold, ritualistic bedrudgeries of outward piety and man-made burdens had weighed down the creature beyond its capacity to endure them.

That zealot of the wilderness known as John the Baptist, echoing the prophetic words of Isaiah, would make a declaration just before the Lord's appearance as He came down that path as the great emancipator from sin. When asked about his credentials and authority that he exercised in order to resound his trumpet of repentance to the mummified masses, his answer would ring with a sweeping truth.

> "Then said they unto him, Who art thou? That we may give an answer to them that sent us. What sayest thou of thyself? He said, I *am* the voice of one crying in the wilderness, make straight the way of the Lord, as said the prophet Esaias." (John 1:22-23 )

This statement by John inevitably raises some questions: What is the **way of the Lord** and, why is it **crooked**? Furthermore, how shall it be **straightened**? If I could indulge in a bit of a paraphrase right here, I think John was saying something like this:

"Clear out the junk of that old religious thinking folks, there's a new game in town! This one is coming to set the record straight between God and man! This one coming is going to remove all those burdensome misconceptions of the divine union between God and man! The kingdom is now **AT HAND.** It's now within your reach and this is about to go ballistic within the interior of man with a dynamo of cleansing fire!"

Oh, glory to God! Imagine these words falling with great authority in the midst of established religion! How it must've shook the earth with a hope, that now, the middleman would be abolished and the commoner could become a priest unto God through the redemptive power of the Spirit! Mankind could now go behind the veil and commune with God through "having our hearts sprinkled from an evil conscience" (see Hebrews 10:22). No more would man need to stay clear of the burning embers of Mount Sinai that sizzled with the law and could not be touched by man nor beast. Conversely, the very embodiment of the law in the man Christ Jesus was here, and we could now ascend Mount Sion and touch the Divine! (see Hebrews 12:18-22).

Yes, this is indeed good news that man could now enter through the forbidden veil and partake of "the riches of the glory of His inheritance in the saints" (see Ephesians 1:18). Jesus purchased not only our salvation through His death, but He also purchased those spiritual blessings, gifts, and graces necessary for the longevity of His church body. These provisions of divine grace would still be functioning among His delegates on the earth, long after His ascension. "Wherefore He saith, when He ascended up on high, He led captivity captive, and gave gifts unto men" (Ephesians 4:8).

Yet, even with all the benefits of Calvary in its glorious demonstration of God's love expressed to broken down and bruised humanity, there can still remain a great disconnect. In Luke chapter 19, we have the account of Jesus passing through Jericho where He would meet a certain fellow whose story was notable enough to make it into the book. The crowds were pressing Jesus to the point of leaving very little space in between

Himself and the many bodies that sought to get a glimpse of Him.

This man called Zacchaeus, would be so earnest to see the Lord, that he would prudently run ahead and find a tree to scale in order to get a birds eye view of the King of all kings. Being small in stature and thereby limited to see over the thronging masses, by climbing this tree, he was now able to lay eyes upon this great wonderment. But, no matter the deficiency, Jesus would **spot him** out of the myriads of seekers and call him down from his privileged perch to abide in his house for the day! Imagine this, Jesus coming for dinner!

However, his occupation, being that of a tax collector, drew the ire of the encroaching crowds to the point of creating a great stir among them.

> "And when they saw *it*, they all murmured, saying, That he was gone to be guest with a man that is a sinner." (Luke 19:7)

When the Lord told Zacchaeus to "Make haste, and come down; for today I must abide at thy house" (vs. 5), he would respond with a torrent of confession and restitutionary zeal. "And Zacchaeus stood, and said unto the Lord; Behold, Lord, the half of my goods I give to the poor; and if I have taken anything from any man by false accusation, I restore *him* fourfold" (vs. 8).

Jesus would waste no time here to put things into their proper perspective. While Zacchaeus was making restitution in his mind to his fellow humans, the Lord was disclosing the bigger picture of making the restitution of man to God! "And Jesus said unto him, This day is salvation come to this house, forasmuch as he also is a son of Abraham" (vs. 9). As the protesting crowds winced at the Lord's desire to tread across the threshold of this despised despot, Jesus would paralyze them with a reality check of the purpose and scope of His mission. "For the Son of man is come to seek and to save that which was lost" (vs. 10).

If we look hard enough in this little account of the Lord's dealings with this tax collector, we can see a hidden gem. Underneath all the fanfare of Zacchaeus' confessional courage, and the clamoring crowds of self-righteousness, was a wonderful truth. This seeking man in the tree, with a hungry heart to see God in the flesh, would hear something a little like this coming from the Lord, if I may paraphrase: "Zacchaeus, you are indeed a sinner, and surely one that is in need of redemption. But I must tell you, it's not what you **give to man or to God** that matters, but what God **gives to you** that counts. **GOD** has come to **seek you** and to retrieve you back to Himself! He is the one who **lost** what was His in the garden and He has come back to claim it!"

I recall some years ago, as I struggled in prayer concerning my own consecration to the Lord and His work, a great truth then dawned upon my soul. I was sweating out my prayers in great angst trying desperately to give my **all** to God. I was pouring over my own soul in great self-examination trying to find the little fragments of spiritual nonconformity that were hidden in the bottom of the barrel of my soul. Many months I wrestled with God, maybe even a year or better, with no resolution in my spirit. I was desperately trying to give God **something, anything** He could use, but I simply did not even know what I was trying to give.

Then one morning in prayer, I heard it. The Lord broke the silence with these life changing words, it's been many years so I will have to paraphrase: "Kenny you have nothing to give me! Every perfect gift cometh down from the Father of lights. The only thing you can truly give me is **A PLACE TO LIVE**! The Son of Man hath not a place to lay **HIS** head. Without me, **YOU** can do **NOTHING!** All I want to do is to dwell **WITHIN** man's temple, it is I that willeth and doeth of my good pleasure within the temple of man's heart."

This moment of clarity would bring me into a new light regarding true consecration. Romans 12 verses 1 and 2 would become, not just a nice couple of verses to quote, but instead, would become a reality that resounded deep within my soul:

> "I beseech you therefore, brethren, by the mercies of God, that ye *present* your bodies a living sacrifice, holy, acceptable unto God, *which is* your reasonable service. And be not conformed to this world: but be ye transformed by the renewing of your mind, that ye may prove what *is* that good, and acceptable, and perfect, will of God." (Romans 12:1-2)

I fear there are millions in this insidious trap of "developmental Christianity" (as I like to call it). Countless multitudes are indeed trying to bring something to God that He simply ***cannot*** use. A consecration that is self-induced, self-prescribed, and self-controlled is no real consecration at all. "Religion," as we may use it here, is that attempted **ascent** of man up into God, while true Christianity is that **descent** of God into man. The difference here, is in fact **THE** difference between, "all things that pertain unto life and godliness" (see 2 Peter 1:3), and the doldrum of servitude that is proceeding from those who are "in the flesh and cannot please God" (see Romans 8:8).

If we become "partakers of the divine nature" (see 2 Peter 1:4) as a result of the indwelling Spirit of God finding residence within our inner temple, we will have all that we need. The goal of the Spirit of God is always fullness! (see Ephesians 3:19). His objective is to fill these earthen vessels to overflowing with the Spirit and nature of His dear Son! He has no other ultimate goal, saving the glorification of Jesus

Christ within the bosom of man. His greatest desire is to fill him with the same, to its most absolute capacity.

Indeed, the **real** good news is this: God is willing to dwell with man in spiritual union and to communicate His very person to us through Christ Jesus! The cross screams "Be ye reconciled unto God!" It shouts, "Be one with me!" It echoes throughout the canyons of eternity with the sweet sound, "I want you back!"

It is the pursuit of God, hot on the trail of the wayfaring sheep, that resounds across the cliffs of the mount of God! "Adam! Where are you? Hide no more among the trees, for I have brought you a remedy! Come, let us fellowship again, for I have provided a sacrifice and will put your sin away!"

Beloved friends, it is the Creator who has suffered the worst loss from the fall. The creature has been created to enjoy his Creator in the fellowship of the cool of the day! It is the creature that has "each gone ***their own way.***" It is we who have become altogether unclean, and it is He who had the nails of that said rebellion driven through His marvelous hands! Those same hands that had healed the sick children of His very killers.

The Lord spoke something to me several years ago that I will never forget. I had been a typical "preacher" and had done my share of pulpit time here and there. Although I had never been a full time pastor, per se, I had at least stammered through a few discourses in various settings at churches, Bible studies, and youth centers alike. One day, as I was simply going about my daily routine, I heard the Lord say this to me, "Kenny, you need to stop preaching the gospel from **man** to God, and start preaching it from **God** to man."

I was a bit taken back initially by such a statement, but as I chewed on those words over the next few months and years, their truth began to slowly unfold in my heart. I began to hear the preaching all around me differently. I started to hear my own preaching differently. While tuning into the essence of modern preaching, through this new discernment of the Holy Spirit, my ears began to open. The more I listened with an open heart, the more I began to hear it. It was none other than a latent sympathy for man's condition in his alienation from God. It was a pity that came from somewhere within the human experience. This preaching had inadvertently painted God as the bad guy, and consequently, man as the pitiful victim of his first fathers fall. For the first time I saw it! It was a backwards gospel!

When we read that poignant piece of lamenting literature deemed "The suffering servant" in Isaiah chapter 53, we find the indictment of man's rebellion, in contrast with God's benevolence. The prophet, while looking through the prophetic scope, would pen some of the most obscure words in the entirety of the book of God. This one "Brought as a lamb to the slaughter" (vs. 7), would possess, "No form nor comeliness; and when we shall see Him, **there is no beauty** that we should desire Him" (vs. 2). This unassuming Nazarite would be "Despised and rejected of men; a man of sorrows, and acquainted with grief: and we hid as it were *our* faces from Him; He was despised, and we esteemed Him not" (vs. 3).

"Surely He hath borne our griefs, and carried our sorrows: yet we did esteem Him stricken, smitten of God, and afflicted" (vs. 4). This humble servant would be "Wounded for our transgressions, *He was* bruised for our iniquities: the chastisement of our peace *was* upon Him; and with His stripes we are healed" (vs. 5).

This brutal account of the rejection of God's Son, and His rescue mission of humanity, has within it a theme that is often overlooked. That is the fact that God cared, when man did not. This ***grief*** and ***sorrow*** that the Lord ***carried*** was making a statement far greater than God just trying to make man happy and to dry his tears. No! This grief is something far greater than that! It is none other than the grief over the sinful and rebellious state that man had morphed into without the divine influence of God in the earth.

This *grief* that the Lord carried was that great *sorrow* of separation between man and the divine which Jesus bore with Him throughout His entire tenure here. It was that same cry He would express as He looked out over that bloody city of Jerusalem and groaned over her insolence for all things good!

> "O Jerusalem, Jerusalem, *thou* that killest the prophets, and stonest them which are sent unto thee, how often would I have gathered thy children together, even as a hen gathereth her chickens under *her* wings, and ye would not!" (Matthew 23:37)

When He would later cry upon the cross those lamenting words of forgiveness, "Father, forgive them for they know not what they do" (Luke 23:34), it would be the culmination of that burden that He carried His whole life! Man had come to despise his very own Creator and Jesus would come and represent an apathetic humanity before the Father with a heart that would cry, "It is finished!" (John 19:30). Man could not even grieve or be sorrowful over his own state, but the Father would send One who would be able to express that lament that we creatures were void of.

Those eyes filled with the blood from those thorns, and that mouth full of vinegar ruthlessly given to Him by His very own creation, would look out over that crowd of those raging bulls and cry out the echo of the sound of the forsaken creature with those words:

> "Eli, Eli, lama sabachthani? That is to say, My God, my God, why hast thou forsaken me?" *(Matthew 27:46)*

Here, many would say that the Father found it necessary to turn His head to avoid **looking at the sin** *that* **was upon** His Son. Indeed, it makes for a good sermon to suggest this, but what was really occurring here? How did He "bare our sins in His own body upon the tree" (see 1 Peter 2:24). I think if we look close enough, we can see something a bit more profound taking place.

If the Lord Jesus was to be a sacrifice *for* **mankind**, He certainly couldn't have gone about it in the sole state of **divinity**. This would have been "cheating" on the part of God to do so. No, this sacrifice had to be fully man. This offering **had to come** from the creature, stripped of all divinity, naked and ashamed, **in the stead** of His otherwise defiled human counterparts. Now, in light of what I just stated, consider these verses:

> "Who, being in the form of God, thought it not robbery to be equal with God: But made Himself of **no reputation**, and took upon Him the *form of a servant*, and was made in the **likeness of men**: And being found in *fashion as a man, He humbled Himself*, and became obedient unto death, even the death of the cross." (Philippians 2:6-8)

Do you see it? **NO REPUTATION! FORM OF A SERVANT! LIKENESS OF MAN!** This is none other than a humility that is beyond human comprehension! A **divine** being laying aside His divinity **voluntarily**, to accomplish redemption as a **man.** This is the mystery of the gospel. There is no doubt in my mind that the Spirit of the Father was succouring His Son through the marring of His visage, the hours of torture, and the endurance of hanging so long in the hot sun. But was there a moment at the end? Was there a moment at the very pinnacle, where **ALL** of the divinity had to step aside, and even the **paraclete** had to depart and leave this ***man*** to gasp for His last breath? Could this be the half hour of silence that John experienced while in the heavenlies? (see Revelation 8:1). Oh my! The thought of such a love! One so voluntary, and disconnected from our selfish state as humans!

How was Jesus able to endure this brutally? It was no doubt possible, due to the fact that He could see something just ahead. "For the joy that was set before Him, He endured the cross, despising the shame" (Hebrews 12:2). That joy was none other than that sweet reconciliation of a lost, unconcerned, disconnected creature that didn't even know the extent of its own wanderings. Oh, let us see it! Let us experience it! And let us enter into its true communion!

> "That I may know Him, and the power of His resurrection, and the fellowship of His sufferings, ***being made conformable unto His death.***" (Philippians 3:10)

Let us come to this soul searching conclusion: All that the Lord wants is a place to live. May He have it so, within our very own bosoms. Let ***HIM*** have what ***HE*** has paid for! Communion with His creature!

> "All we like sheep have gone astray; we have turned every one to his own way; and the LORD hath laid on Him the iniquity of us all." (Isaiah 53:6)

I think it is fitting that we end this chapter with the old Moravian slogan. "May the Lamb that was slain, receive the reward of His suffering!!!"

Chapter 22

# THE REMNANT RISING

*"And I heard another voice from heaven, saying,
Come out of her, my people, that ye be not partakers of her
sins, and that ye recieve not of her plagues." Revelation 18:4*

I'VE BEEN IN THE FLOOR COVERING BUSINESS most of my life and I have dealt with hundreds of pieces of carpet known as "remnants." These little forgotten fragments that have been left over from the larger rolls are typically bundled up, set aside, and (seemingly) marked at a reduced price. The problem with remnants is just that, they are remnants, and being a small part of the greater whole, are unique in size. Their application is typically very much limited, due to their size and color. I have seen remnants sit in the corner, or on a rack, for upwards of 20 years without finding someone to walk on them. These homeless has-beens of the carpet world find themselves being marked further and further down in price in order to be liquidated, and consequently, make room for the new stock that would replace them.

But then, one day it happens! Susie homemaker walks in on the scene with her samples of a couch cushion and choice wall coverings looking for a perfect match for her sunroom. The carpet that is in her room currently is old and soiled. Not to mention that Clarabelle, her beloved aging retriever, has unfortunately mistaken it for the yard on several occasions. She's on a budget, in a hurry, and has no time for ordered goods. She has uncle Marvin and aunt Janean coming in for the weekend and she knows how much they like to sit in that room with all the windows and watch the bustling bird feeder.

She meanders around the carpet store peering earnestly at the stock pile of remnants. She meticulously lays her samples of paint and the couch cushion on several selections, but finds that they are either off color, way too large, or way too small for her application. She's just about to give up and traverse through the midtown traffic over to Barney's Basement Bargains to check out his selection, when she spots it! There, in the corner, hidden in obscurity, marked down even below reasonable logic, is her little remnant! The perfect match and the perfect size! Her excitement is tangible and she becomes ecstatic over the bounty of her great find within the forgotten mines of those remnant rations. Her little chosen one from the corner is installed the next day, and the room is quickly set back up for visitors. Susie is now a most grateful and satisfied customer.

Just as Susie homemaker overlooked the newest **popular** style and went for that little forgotten remnant, the Lord is always up to something behind the scenes of the bigger picture. While we are focused on the *full roll*, and the **latest styles**, God is focused on the little piece at the end, that seemingly unusable **remnant.**

When we see the size and scope of the modern church with all her drapings and drama, it gives us great pause. We are witnessing entire denominations voting against the very foundational principles of the Word of God, coupled with many fallen religious leaders, and not to mention, an equally apostate pew. When we take in all of this, we are left to ask: If these folks are the representatives of God, then who's right here? If everyone thinks they are the truth holders, where does that leave everyone else? Is God in all of this confusion anywhere? These are indeed legitimate questions that swirl around our everyday lifestyles to one degree or another.

Religion in America is that 800 lb gorilla in the room. Ignore it as one may try, yet it is always there as a fixture in the western mindset. Like it or not, modern Christianity encircles every single facet of our lives, from government, all the way down to the common workplace. So, while mankind is trampling their way through the local landfills of nominal Christianity, searching for something legitimate within all the rubbage of the religious rhetoric, God is working behind the scenes.

We must ask: What does a last day remnant look like? How could one know if they have found it? How can a person know if they are in it or not? If they are not in it, how do they become a part of it? All of these questions can and should be answered for every true, **hungry** God seeker. It is the earmark of the last days church and her overcoming longevity depends on the definitive elements of this *"**called out**"* assembly of true soldiers of the cross.

When we think about our opening text and the Lord's call to "Come out of **her** my people and receive not of **her** plagues" (see Revelation 18:4), we are then obligated to know who the "**her**" is. In our previous chapters, I believe we have established that this "queen of continual corruption" is none other than a religion that has been concocted in a cauldron of deceptive ingredients. Satan has worked the perfect angles, through the perfect specimen, to make the perfect hybrid of a counterfeit Christianity.

One thing we know of a certainty, this calling out from under this woman's influence and power, will lead one away from the effects of a "plague." I believe this plague must certainly be a ***spiritual death*** of sorts that has fallen like a mist on all who remain in her diabolical clutches. Any form of Christianity that seeks to allow the "old man" within us to stay alive and to operate covertly under the guise of the true religion of Jesus Christ, is indeed the religion of an antichrist (substitute) spirit.

Now, to answer those questions we asked earlier, what does this **remnant** look like, how do you know you are in it, and, if not, how does one enter it?

One of the attributes of this separated stock is its reduced popularity among the *"in crowd"* of modern religion. Like that little carpet remnant that Susie chose, they have been reduced through rejection time and time again, and placed in the corner of obscurity. They have within them an inherited, innate sort of peculiarity that distinguishes them from the larger circle. Like the *wallflower* at the high school dance, they just never seem to fit into anything of the norm with even a semblance of comfort. Their attempts to conform to anything other than their own rejected kind, only brings them into more angst and introversion. Their anthem rings, not on the overt stages of the limelight, but in the hidden amphitheaters of their own heart. It is the sound of separation, and the psalm of solitude.

While the crowds of conformity are searching for a king like Saul, "A choice young man, and a goodly: and there was not among the children of Israel a goodlier person than he: from his shoulders and upward he was higher than any of the people" (see 1 Samuel 9:2), the Lord is searching the pastures for one who is "ruddy" and reliable such as a David (see 1 Samuel 16:12). While the masses clamor for the most aesthetically pleasing specimen from the stock, God has His own man of obscurity, hidden on the hillsides of humility, tending to the sheep.

Typically speaking, what man elevates, God views with disdain. "For that which is highly esteemed among men is abomination in the sight of God" (see Luke 16:15). Man's tendency to make his calculations from the amalgamation of his five senses, almost always ends in disaster. As was the case with Saul, one who was "higher than any of the people" who seemed to fit the part. But lurking in the bosom of this "giant among men" was a bubbling cauldron of compromise. Oh, you can never see it while he is being paraded before the thronging crowds as the representative darling of the disenfranchised. The people always have the tendency to choose what best represents **them**, but the Lord sees through the latent layers of perceived piety, and zeroes in on the lowliness and meekness of a man that best represents **Him**. "For man looketh on the outward appearance, but the Lord looketh on the heart" (see 1 Samuel 16:7).

We must keep in mind that this disconnected king was a product of the people. He was the symbol of a people who wanted to "heap to themselves" a personal representative to spring them from the oppression of their enemies. This clamoring for a king came in the vacuum of Samuels own two sons failing to fulfill their leadership as judges (see 1st Samuel 8:3), combined with the desire of the children of Israel to have a semblance of the **structured** nations around them.

> "Then all the elders of Israel gathered themselves together, and came to Samuel unto Ramah, And said unto him, Behold, thou art old, and thy sons walk not in thy ways: now ***make us a king*** to judge us like all the nations. But the thing displeased Samuel, when they said, Give us a king to judge us. And Samuel prayed unto the Lord." (1st Samuel 8:4-6)

"Make us a king!" Oh the danger of this request! "Kingmakers" abound in the realm of the discontented and desperate. This great lack of leadership is the incubator for vanity and tyranny. It is in this vacuum of mankind's clamoring need for a ruler over him, where narcissistic leaders are born. ***"Kingly kings"*** that are chosen by man, seldom make it for the long haul because they typically self-implode with their perversion of power, as did Saul. Conversely, **"lowly leaders"** are in it for the duration of a thing because they know their place among men stems from a much higher cause than themselves.

If we look hard enough, there is a *type* here for the modern church to observe and learn from. It is the fact that there is a vast difference between a man voted in by human *consensus,* and a man ordained through the *consent* of heaven. The modern church's model of manmade "selective service" methodologies, looks much like a poster of Uncle Sam pointing out to the masses, looking for a "few *good* men." We are pumping out preachers from the factories of "higher learning" at an alarming rate. Rolling them out as a ready-made product to be moved about from one congregation to another, based on nothing else but demographics, voting power, and the ability to gel with their sheep.

After Saul's disastrous disobedience early in his reign as king, the lamenting prophet Samuel would cry throughout the night at such a loss and disappointment in the one he had anointed as the people's representative. God would express this same disappointment and regret to Samuel himself in regards to Sauls rebellious insolence towards Him:

> "It repenteth me that I have set up Saul to be king: for he is turned back from following me, and hath not performed my commandments. And it grieved Samuel; and he cried unto the Lord all night." (1 Samuel 15:11)

God is ever moving forward in His ideals. The misgivings and missteps of His creatures never deter Him from His mission. He may very well grieve over the losses, but He is ever working in the hearts of men and women, searching for those who will join Him in His great mission of recovery of "that which was lost." He never ceases from His conquest of consecration. "For the eyes of the LORD run to and fro throughout the whole earth, to shew Himself strong in the behalf of *them* whose heart *is* perfect toward Him" (see 2 Chronicles 16:9). He would call Samuel out of the lamentations of the past, basically telling him to "press toward the mark, forgetting those things which are behind" (see Philippians 3:13-14).

> "And the Lord said unto Samuel, How long wilt thou mourn for Saul, seeing I have rejected him from reigning over Israel? Fill thine horn with oil, and go, I will send thee to Jesse the Bethlehemite: For I have provided me a king among his sons." (1 Samuel 16:1)

We must always move forward, because God always moves forward. The king Davids are always in the wings, and the Lord will continue pressing forth the mission of having men and women after His own heart. The Lord would tell Samuel to take his oil and go to a man with many sons, to find that one in the stock to represent **Him,** and not the **people**. "I will send thee to Jesse the Bethlehemite: for ***I have provided me a king*** among his sons," (1 Samuel 16:1). Here, David surely represents that hidden thing: that undercurrent of meekness and dependency on God that only comes from years on the hillsides with lambs and encroaching wolves. This is where men of God are grown, and not manufactured. With sheep dung on their sandals, and a melody in their heart, they have learned God under the stars, and there, learned the emptiness of personal stardom.

In chapter 16, when Samuel arrived at Jesse's place, he would have the stock of Jesse's sons paraded before him in order to "size them up." The Lord would tell him to take a heifer and sacrifice it there (vs. 2), calling Jesse and his sons to the event (vs. 3). Immediately, Samuels five senses would kick in as he spotted one of the sons and would feel that, "knowing" in his mind that he had indeed found the **one!**

"And it came to pass, when they were come, that he looked on Eliab, and said, **Surely** the Lord's anointed is before him." (vs. 6)

No sooner had this thought rose up in Samuel and pressed to his lips for confirmation, when the Lord chided him for **almost** committing the same sin as when Saul was selected from among the stock! Oh, how quick we are to feel a thing out with our human sensibilities!

"But the Lord said unto Samuel, **Look not** on his **countenance**, or on the height of his stature; because I have refused him: for the **Lord seeth not as man seeth**; for man looketh on the outward appearance, but the Lord looketh on the heart." (vs. 7)

Oh, what a test this was for the man of God! Seven sons would pass by without a confirmation! Samuel had to indeed question himself at this point. What happened to my "knower"? It seems to be not working, did I grieve the Lord here? Did I miss it altogether? Not wanting to insult the dear father, he would have likely asked this next question with reservation: "Are here all thy children?" (vs. 11) Jesse would reply almost in disbelief after parading such a fine stock of specimens before the prophet: And he said, "There remaineth yet the youngest, and, behold, he **keepeth the sheep**." And Samuel said unto Jesse, "Send and fetch him: for we will not sit down till he come hither" (vs. 11).

At this point, Samuel's "knower" began to work again. There is just that ***divine*** thing that happens, and you know it when it does. It's when God truly sets His approval on something and puts His stamp on a moment in time, along with a certain person within that moment. This was one of those instances. Samuel likely found himself a bit relieved that there was yet another and he then knew in his heart of certainty, he had found the ***one*** this time. Jesse called for the boy to come forth from the sheepfold and young David sauntered into the event as a wallflower, an outcast, and a rejected remnant! But, God alone knew where he fit, God alone knew his heart, and God alone knew His intentions with this one. "And he sent, and brought him in. Now he was ruddy, and withal of a beautiful countenance, and goodly to look to. And the Lord said, Arise, anoint him: for this is he" (vs. 12).

There it was, as if standing before all the ingenuity of man, and standing against the surmisings of this world, a man chosen directly by God based on nothing but sheer affection between the man and his Lord. This young, undesirable lad had no prowess, no seniority, no high place in the pecking order, and no learned skills of academia. Just a ruddy, red-headed shepherd boy with the skills of a harpist and the pen of a heavenly orator! What we see here in David, is indeed the essence of the remnant that God always sets aside for Himself. This is no doubt the heart of God expressed in this simple example of a boy who did not just know ***about*** God, but in fact, was known ***by*** his God!

Like our dear young David, this inconspicuous band of ardent seekers called the ***remnant*** are but interested in one thing, the perfect will of God! Strangely, they are somehow magnetized to one another by that inner metal of their collective hunger for all things holy and righteous within the nature of their God. There is an unseen, cohesive element that glues them to one another in the labyrinth of spiritual union. It's like a spider's web strewn across the great expanse of time and space, tapped into the sensitivity of God's heart. When He moves, they move. When He doesn't, they wait.

No, these "parts of the whole" are not looking for a way to have their **spiritual cake and eat it too.** They are not looking for doctrinal diversions to confirm their own self-absorbed destiny. These are the ones who have set among the numbed numbers with their Sunday morning complacency and have "weighed it all in the balance and have found it to be wanting."

This rogue band of zealots can never, ever, settle for mediocrity. They have been to the mount and have seen a God that scorches the top of it with a nature separate and most glorious. They can never settle into a place where normalcy reigns supreme. Neither can they ever deny that the Lord's expression of Himself is always greater, more expansive, and decidedly opulent beyond anything that they can "ask or think" (see Ephesians 3:20). The measuring rod of these separated sentinels is the unlimited resources of a limitless God. They know that something yet remains, something further must unfold, and something must still culminate to the ultimate glory of God. They are waiting, watching and expecting an outpouring of unprecedented proportions. In the book of Malachi, we see the earmarks of this remnant. It is unveiled there as a distinctive entity, with true reverential fear, set apart within God's own heart as the crown jewels of His creation.

> "Then they that feared the LORD spake often one to another: and the LORD hearkened, and heard *it*, and a book of remembrance was written before Him for them that feared the LORD, and that thought upon His name. And they shall be mine, saith the LORD of hosts, in that day when I make up my jewels; and I will spare them, as a man spareth His

own son that serveth Him. Then shall ye return, and discern between the righteous and the wicked, between him that serveth God and him that serveth Him not." (Malachi 3:16-18)

In order to belong to this remnant (or to be initiated into it), is not something you necessarily ***do***, as much as it is something you ***are***. If you are a part of this wonderful fold, peculiarity is the mark on your soul, and the Lord makes this promise to you:

"To him that overcometh will I give to eat of the hidden manna, and will give him a white stone, and in the stone a new name written, which no man knoweth saving he that receiveth *it*." (Revelation 2:17)

A glorious church will arise in this last hour, she may not be large in size, but she will be a giant in the fruit of certainty. She will not be confused with her predecessors of peddled man-made piety. The radiance of her gown will be bristling white with the purity of her chastity for her groom and this distinction will set her apart from all other religious regalities. This church will be a spontaneous specimen of spiritual combustion in which "fire proceedeth out of their mouth, and devoureth their enemies." Her witness will be the fact that she has ***indeed seen something***, she will not get her info second hand, or from "one fallen head to another fallen head." She will fulfill a repeat of the book of Acts, only more so. The iniquity that has abounded in this world is calling for more grace still. The times demand her to rise, she cannot but come from her bride chambers aglow with heavenly affection. It is the reason she was purchased, and her entire sole purpose is to be espoused to her groom in spotless matrimony. She will in turn radiate the splendor of their coronation, a union, in which, was purchased by blood.

Dear friends, let us heed that admonition from the apostle Peter to "give diligence to make your calling and election sure" (2 Peter 1:10). Let us equally take heed to Paul's warning to "examine yourselves, whether ye be in the faith" (2 Corinthians 13:5). And let us never forget that "the Lord knoweth them that are His. And, Let everyone that nameth the name of Christ depart from iniquity" (2 Timothy 2:19). We end this book with a promise and a proclamation. As the Great Whore of religion sinks into oblivion, the Lord **WILL** have a bride that is His reflection in the earth!

As the moon is to the sun.......

So shall she be!

"That He might sanctify and cleanse it with the washing of water by the Word, That He might present it to Himself a glorious church, not having spot, or wrinkle, or any such thing; but that it should be holy and without blemish." (Ephesians 5:26-27)

So be it!

# EPILOGUE

Towards the end of the writing of *Bats in the Bell Tower* my wife approached me one day with elation upon her countenance. She spoke in her typical boisterous way when the things of God excite her spirit and cause her to burst at the seams with the desire to share her revelations and findings. I looked up from the keyboard with great expectation as I was all too familiar with that look after 35 years of knowing her. She gave me her typical question, "Can I read you something?" As if I could ever say no to such a statement! One thing I know most assuredly about my wife, when she has something of godly persuasion on her heart, it is always good to take advantage of the moment. I can never, within the confines of my memory, remember hearing her babble senselessly about spiritual things.

She began to read the following account to me and I was quite taken aback by it. Tears filled my eyes as I felt the movings of God upon my heart. A short time later, our neighbors Brett and Kelsey came to visit us. Again, my dear wife brought up her story to them and asked if they wanted to hear what she wrote. They of course gave a collective,

"Sure, let's hear it!" After she was done reading it, we all just kind of expressed the collective, "Wow, that's awesome!" I spoke up and said, "We have to find a way to get this in the book, it just has too much of the touch of God upon it not to include it." Brett and Kelsey both testified that the same thought had come into their mind when she was done reading it. Therefore, "In the mouth of 2 or 3 witnesses," the determination was made for its entry into this book.

The following words are not an *epilogue* in the classic sense of the word, yet regardless, it helps us end with an exclamation point. They are a simple account of an experience with God and His power to save. The message in the great book of God is really comprised of the following three central elements that distinguish them one from another: When God does something within mankind, when mankind does something without God, or, when mankind and the Devil do something together. The following story from my dear wife is just such an example of when God does something within a person! We hope you are edified.

The absolute best day of my life was in 1986, I was 16 years old, and yeah, that was a long time ago but yet it is still the most vivid, monumental, eye-opening and euphoric day that I have ever experienced. I never knew such a feeling like that even existed. Maybe people expect me to say that the best day was my wedding day or the days of my children's birth, it was neither of those nor was it simply fortuitous in nature. Those days were beautiful and exciting, days and experiences that I treasure deeply and always will. What I'm about to say doesn't take away from any people in my life whether friends or family, so there's no need to get offended, but there is something even greater. Most people don't even know of its existence, yet they fight it and even run from it like it's the black death. I'll try to take the reader on this journey with me, back to the fall of 1986, I'll bare my soul to you if you will take the time to read on.

I felt so empty, isolated and alone. I really don't know even how to describe the inner pain that I had, it was a despair that never left, crippling me, beating me down, causing me to want to destroy myself but too afraid of hell to do so. I found no comfort in anyone, not one soul. I had discovered that I was never going to get what I wanted out of people, relationships, my quest for success and money or a party lifestyle. It was all empty, and it only left me feeling more and more void. Maybe some of you, if not all, can relate right now but even if you can't, keep reading because this story does escalate to a pivotal point of divine satisfaction.

So, on a particular mediocre and dull day in the fall of '86 my mother received a phone call from my cousin. He had a narrative to tell of a friend of his that had gone through a monumental and drastic change in his life, all for the good. It was clear that he held this individual in high esteem because he had shared a friendship with him for several years and knew his life personally. This was not just some whim his friend was going through, it was much too radical and deep for that. He spoke with much exuberance and desire to bring this friend over for a conversation concerning this change and how it had such a big effect on himself and others around him. I had never heard him sound so enlivened.

So the day came and my cousin brought this young man along with one more to our house to talk with my mom and I. The fellow was only 20 years old, incidentally. For some reason unknown to us, we were feeling an odd anticipation as we approached the front door and eagerly opened it. In walked my cousin, another one of their friends, and the future writer of this book. Instantly I felt anger that I did not understand when I looked at this gentleman for the first time in my life. I'm thinking, wow, where did this come from?! I was sure that I had never felt like this when meeting a new person and it stunned me and jolted the arrogant, fake confidence that I had. My mom welcomed them in as I proceeded to keep my distance as I was also feeling this fear of sorts. The conversation that followed was mostly between my mother and this fellow as I listened in from the sidelines. I would step into the room briefly then step back away again but never leaving to a point where the dialogue was inaudible.

The discourse was entirely upon who God was and His dealings with mankind. This made me substantially uneasy and uncomfortable. My feelings just confused me further because I had longed to know God from the tender young age of five, so where was all of this coming from? I had no answers but only felt the strong urge to argue with the man and prove him wrong. He did, however, maintain his calm and peaceable demeanor in spite of all my efforts to destroy it. They left several hours later and I was forced to really look at myself in the mirror. All of my hostile words towards him were met with the soft, gentle nature of Jesus Himself within this man although I didn't understand that at the time.

I spent the next 2 weeks thinking heavily upon all that was said and finally came to the conclusion that he had what my desperate soul had been searching for and with every ounce of my being I decided I was going to get what he had. I could not deny the peace, it was almost tangible and a deposit of it was left there when he departed. Hope was indeed hovering. Later on, this man made a phone call to our house that I overheard and he spoke of a church that he was attending. With every fiber of my being I wanted to go, I felt desperate and somehow

# EPILOGUE

I knew this was the path that I was to take. So, shortly thereafter, on a chilled, autumn Sunday morning, my cousin arrived to pick me up and take me to this congregation. We met up with the two that had been to our house and then went on to the high school auditorium where this group met for services.

That daybreak felt different before I even got there. I felt it in the morning air, sensed it in the dew, experienced it in the warming rays of the sun.....what was it? It was the very essence of God Himself, manifesting in His creation. I walked in that old high school auditorium with a sense of elation and expectancy I had never known before. The voices had already joined together in unison, singing with sweet sounds of joy and love as choir and congregation sang out in perfect harmony. I found a seat, placed my purse and Bible on the floor and attempted to sit down but was not able to do so. Instantly, I shot straight up out of the chair, raised my hands in the air and joined the glorious praise unto God. As my voice went up to Him, my heart went out in ravenous hunger as I feasted upon the majesty of the presence of Almighty God. In that moment, all pain, worry, fear, and bitterness left me and the void was completely filled with love and joy beyond human comprehension. In that moment, my sins were forgiven and I was "born-again." The book of John (1:12-13) explains it this way, "But as many as received Him, to them gave He power to become the sons (and daughters) of God, even to them that believe on His name, which were born, not of blood, nor of the will of the flesh, nor of the will of man, but of God."

At this point I'm sure most who are reading this are thinking, wow that's so great for you! But, there's something else that you must realize for yourself and that is, you must have an experience with God yourself, where you go from darkness to light and everything about you changes. Do you believe Jesus was a truth teller when He said, "Except a man be born again he cannot enter the kingdom of heaven?" (see John Ch.3). It's not some empty prayer you speak with nothing behind it and no commitment on your part. There will be a significant, dramatic and noticeable change within you or nothing has taken place at all. Please don't cheat yourself by discarding my words, there is no greater experience in life than knowing God intimately and there's only one way to get it. You've got to settle your account with God by turning from your old life and embracing a new one with the Divine Being that created you. What you do with this will decide your eternal abode.

This world is in absolute chaos and distress, who can deny that? It's on a downward spiral that can not be reversed, and at the end of it all, it's pointless and holds no real eternal value. Let us take heed to the words of Solomon and his wisdom.....Ecclesiastes 12:1 says "Remember now your Creator in the days of your youth, while the evil days come not, nor the years draw nigh, when you shall say, I have no pleasure in them." And also, Ecclesiastes 12:13-14 says "Let us hear the conclusion of the whole matter: Fear God and keep His commandments, for this is the whole duty of man. For God shall bring every work into judgment, with every secret thing, whether it be good, or whether it be evil."

There's another verse in the Bible that I want the reader to be aware of:

It's found in 1 John 5:12.... "He that has the Son has life, and he that has not the Son has not life." Remember, He came to seek and to save that which was lost and He didn't come to condemn the world, but that the world might be saved through Him.

May this book and this testimony birth in you a desire to know the truth, receive the truth, believe on Him for salvation, and receive His fullness. If you will, you will also be that voice echoing, PREPARE YE THE WAY OF THE LORD!!!

# EPILOGUE

"Behold He cometh with clouds; and every eye shall see Him. And they also which pierced Him. And all kindreds of the earth shall wail because of Him. Even so. Amen. I am Alpha and Omega, the beginning and the ending, saith the Lord, which is, and which was, and which is to come, the Almighty. (Revelation 1:7-8)

Milton Keynes UK
Ingram Content Group UK Ltd.
UKHW020614080823
426502UK00013B/357